HARPER TORCHBOOKS

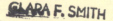

Rachel Bespaloff	ON THE ILIAD. Introduction
Elliott Coleman, *ed.*	LECTURES IN CRITICISM: *By ~~~~~~~~~~~~~~~* Crowe Ransom, Herbe~
C. G. Jung	PSYCHOLOGICAL REFLECTIONS
Erich Neumann	THE ORIGINS AND HISTORY ~~~~~~~~~~~~ II, TB/2008
St.-John Perse	SEAMARKS. Translated by Wallace Fowlie TB/2002
Jean Seznec	THE SURVIVAL OF THE PAGAN GODS: *The Mythological Tradition and Its Place in Renaissance Humanism and Art.* Illustrated TB/2004
Heinrich Zimmer	MYTHS AND SYMBOLS IN INDIAN ART AND CIVILIZATION TB/2005

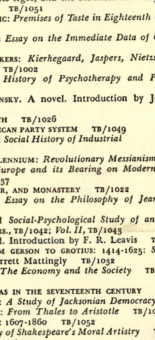

HARPER TORCHBOOKS / The Academy Library

James Baird	ISHMAEL: *A Study of the Symbolic Mode in Primitivism* TB/1023
Herschel Baker	THE IMAGE OF MAN: *A Study of the Idea of Human Dignity in Classical Antiquity, the Middle Ages, and the Renaissance* TB/1047
Jacques Barzun	THE HOUSE OF INTELLECT TB/1051
W. J. Bate	FROM CLASSIC TO ROMANTIC: *Premises of Taste in Eighteenth Century England* TB/1036
Henri Bergson	TIME AND FREE WILL: *An Essay on the Immediate Data of Consciousness* TB/1021
H. J. Blackham	SIX EXISTENTIALIST THINKERS: *Kierkegaard, Jaspers, Nietzsche, Marcel, Heidegger, Sartre* TB/1002
Walter Bromberg	THE MIND OF MAN: *A History of Psychotherapy and Psychoanalysis* TB/1003
Abraham Cahan	THE RISE OF DAVID LEVINSKY. A novel. Introduction by John Higham TB/1028
Helen Cam	ENGLAND BEFORE ELIZABETH TB/1026
Joseph Charles	THE ORIGINS OF THE AMERICAN PARTY SYSTEM TB/1049
T. C. Cochran & William Miller	THE AGE OF ENTERPRISE: *A Social History of Industrial America* TB/1054
Norman Cohn	THE PURSUIT OF THE MILLENNIUM: *Revolutionary Messianism in Medieval and Reformation Europe and its Bearing on Modern Totalitarian Movements* TB/1037
G. G. Coulton	MEDIEVAL VILLAGE, MANOR, AND MONASTERY TB/1022
Wilfrid Desan	THE TRAGIC FINALE: *An Essay on the Philosophy of Jean-Paul Sartre* TB/1030
Cora Du Bois	THE PEOPLE OF ALOR: *A Social-Psychological Study of an East Indian Island. Vol. I,* 85 illus., TB/1042; *Vol. II,* TB/1043
George Eliot	DANIEL DERONDA. A novel. Introduction by F. R. Leavis TB/1039
John N. Figgis	POLITICAL THOUGHT FROM GERSON TO GROTIUS: 1414-1625: *Seven Studies.* Introduction by Garrett Mattingly TB/1032
Editors of *Fortune*	AMERICA IN THE SIXTIES: *The Economy and the Society* TB/1015
F. L. Ganshof	FEUDALISM TB/1058
G. P. Gooch	ENGLISH DEMOCRATIC IDEAS IN THE SEVENTEENTH CENTURY TB/1006
Francis J. Grund	ARISTOCRACY IN AMERICA: *A Study of Jacksonian Democracy* TB/1001
W. K. C. Guthrie	THE GREEK PHILOSOPHERS: *From Thales to Aristotle* TB/1008
Marcus Lee Hansen	THE ATLANTIC MIGRATION: 1607-1860 TB/1052
Alfred Harbage	AS THEY LIKED IT: *A Study of Shakespeare's Moral Artistry* TB/1035
J. M. Hussey	THE BYZANTINE WORLD TB/1057
Henry James	THE PRINCESS CASAMASSIMA. A novel. Intro. by Clinton Oliver. TB/1005
Henry James	RODERICK HUDSON. A novel. Introduction by Leon Edel TB/1016
Henry James	THE TRAGIC MUSE. A novel. Introduction by Leon Edel TB/1017
William James	PSYCHOLOGY: *The Briefer Course.* Edited with an Introduction by Gordon Allport TB/1034
Arnold Kettle	AN INTRODUCTION TO THE ENGLISH NOVEL. *Vol. I, Defoe to George Eliot,* TB/1011; *Vol. II, Henry James to the Present,* TB/1012
Samuel Noah Kramer	SUMERIAN MYTHOLOGY: *A Study of Spiritual and Literary Achievement in the Third Millennium B.C.* Illustrated TB/1055
Paul Oskar Kristeller	RENAISSANCE THOUGHT: *The Classic, Scholastic, and Humanist Strains* TB/1048
L. S. B. Leakey	ADAM'S ANCESTORS: *The Evolution of Man and His Culture.* Illustrated TB/1019
Bernard Lewis	THE ARABS IN HISTORY TB/1029
Ferdinand Lot	THE END OF THE ANCIENT WORLD AND THE BEGINNINGS OF THE MIDDLE AGES TB/1044

HARPER TORCHBOOKS / The Cloister Library

A Life of Jesus

by

EDGAR J. GOODSPEED

HARPER TORCHBOOKS

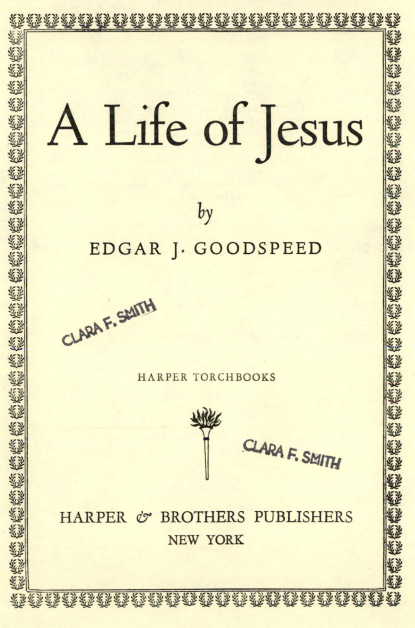

HARPER & BROTHERS PUBLISHERS
NEW YORK

In ever loving memory of

ELFLEDA

1880–1949

who asked me to write this book

CONTENTS

Preface

"The life of Jesus Christ cannot be written." This has long been a commonplace with historians and biographers.

And yet what life has been so often written? Not, indeed, with the precision and fullness of information the ideal biography demands, and yet more movingly and tellingly than any other person's history. For the story of Jesus and how he flashed like a meteor across the sky of his generation and this world cannot be told too often. Adequately it can indeed never be written, but though all other life stories fade from the memory of men, it must never be forgotten, for its sheer influence on human thought, human relations and human destiny, and for its incomparable contribution to man's faith in good and goodness. But who is sufficient for these things?

No biography of Jesus can be written without emotion. To try to do so is to miss what is basic and central in it all. For it is a record of great emotions—of commission, temptation, devotion, compassion, surrender and sacrifice. If one is a stranger to these emotions, he can never penetrate to the meaning of Jesus' life and ministry, for he was a man of great emotions.

But of course they were more than emotions; they were convictions. And anyone who is a stranger to convictions

Introduction

The earthly life of Jesus has come down to us in the records of the four gospels of Matthew, Mark, Luke and John, with some secondary echoes in a score or more of later, uncanonical gospels, of most of which only fragments now exist. These last are, however, so obviously based on the first four that they present no substantial addition to them except a striking saying or two, which may possibly be authentic.

Of the original four, John is the latest, and the most obviously Greek in origin, being an admirable effort to present the great religious values of the new faith in terms immediately intelligible to the Greek mind. Its emphasis is upon the Christian's religious experience of Jesus as a spiritual force. It is therefore of immense importance as evidence of his spiritual influence, rather than of the course of events during his life on earth. Its doctrines are strongly influenced by the collected letters of Paul, and it was written probably in the circle of Ephesus early in the second century after Christ. Very soon after its publication, the gospels were collected by Christian enterprise, and published, notwithstanding their differences, as a collection, forming, we may fairly say, the most successful piece of publishing in all history, since no other publishing

of scenes only Peter, James and John are present; at Caesarea Philippi it is Peter who speaks up to answer Jesus'
question, and who rebukes Jesus, and is rebuked; and of
his three denials at the trial only Peter could have known
and told.

I Peter, written probably about A.D. 95, speaks in behalf
of "your sister church in Babylon and Mark my son."
Babylon is the regular apocalyptic name for Rome, in the
Revelation, Baruch, the Letter of Jeremiah and II Esdras,
in the Apocrypha. Mark was not Peter's son, except in the
figurative, spiritual sense, and the coupling of Mark, Peter
and Rome together can hardly point to anything less than
the recording of Peter's testimony, by Mark, in Rome.
I Peter 5:13 is in effect an allusion to what we know as
the Gospel of Mark, as embodying the reminiscences of
Peter and as emanating from the church at Rome. When
it is remembered that I Peter was written to save the
churches of Asia Minor from the vengeful attitude toward
their persecutors which the Revelation of John seemed to
inculcate (18:6, 20; compare I Peter 2:13-17; 3:8, 9), it
will be seen that the church at Rome needed all the authority it could muster to offset the exalted claims of direct
inspiration made in the Revelation of John.

Thus the incidental external evidence as to the origin
of Mark (except for the probable presence of a "little
apocalypse" in Chapter 13) agrees very well with the
internal evidence which the book itself gives as to its
probable origin.

The Gospel of Mark presents Jesus as a Doer, a Man

46:7, Polycarp's Letter to the Philippians 2:3. Things taken from it are usually introduced with the words "Remember the words of the Lord Jesus," or "remembering what the Lord said in his teaching."

It was in this incipient form that the gospel story was known to Paul and quoted in I Corinthians 11:24, 25, verses which give us our oldest account of the Last Supper, and 15:5, 6, so important as the earliest account of the Resurrection.

The writings of Paul and the evangelists were only the beginning of a great writing movement on the part of the early Christians, and these writings were widely circulated and read among the churches, so that there was much interpretation of Jesus' teaching and of his life and death, and development of these interpretations in the books that followed, in the New Testament, the so-called Apostolic Fathers, the writings of the Christian defenders of the new religion, the apologists, and the resisters of schismatic and sectarian movements, such as that of Marcion about A.D. 140.

The death of Jesus, which at first seemed so bitterly to disappoint all the high Messianic hopes of his followers of a redeemed nation, which should lead the world into the kingdom of God, in the light of what he had said at the Last Supper, and of their new experience of his continued presence, took on a new and grander meaning. It was a great sacrifice, the Son of God offering himself up for the sins of mankind. This idea was suggested by Jesus' words at the Supper, when he spoke of his body as taking

Tremendous developments had already taken place. But fortunately such is the wealth of early Christian literature during the preceding century and a half that we can trace their progress. For this we cannot be too grateful. This literature was wholly Greek, for it was only where the Christian movement entered the Greek world, of books and writers, that it began to express itself in writing (A.D. 50), in letters and then in books. Meantime, Aramaic-speaking Judaism with its avowed aversion to religious writing and its dependence on oral tradition went on its nonliterary way for a hundred and fifty years.

Yet we can even from what survives in the Mishnah recover something of the rabbinical background—the views of Shammai and Hillel—against which Jesus' teaching is silhouetted.

Josephus, the Jewish historian, who wrote his *Antiquities of the Jews* in Rome under Domitian, A.D. 81-96, finishing it in A.D. 93, speaks of Jesus twice, once casually, in *Antiquities* xx.9. 1, in connection with the stoning of James "the brother of Jesus who was called Christ" at the instigation of the high priest Ananus (Annas). The longer passage, which is found in *Antiquities* xviii.3. 3, reads thus:

"There arose at this time Jesus a wise man, if it is right to call him a man. For he was a doer of extraordinary acts, a teacher of men who are glad to receive the truth, and he drew to himself many Jews and many of the Greek race. He was the Christ. And when Pilate at the instance of the foremost men among us had sentenced him to be cruci-

centuries. To some their evidence is disappointing, it is so small and casual. But it must be remembered that they wrote for the Roman world, a world so far removed from the kingdom of heaven which Jesus sought to inaugurate that it is a wonder they ever even mentioned him at all. It is hard for us moderns, in America at least, to envisage that Roman world, so brutal, callous, cruel, coarse. It was a world of slavery; if the slaves in it did not outnumber the free people, they came very near it. When Corinth was captured by Lucius Mummius in 146 B.C., the whole population was sold into slavery. Many of these slaves were better-educated people than their masters. The Romans thought nothing of crucifying people by the thousand. They found entertainment in seeing men and wild animals fight each other to death. Augustus in his *Res Gestae*, his "Achievements" composed for his epitaph by himself, as many scholars believe, reported that ten thousand men had fought in gladiatorial shows given the Roman public by him. He was proud of it. Unwanted babies were thrown out to die; kindhearted persons who picked them up and reared them could have them, or sell them, as slaves. In the latter part of the first century the most popular humorist at Rome was a man whose epigrams are many of them so obscene that modern publishers will not print them in translation. To such a world Jesus would not appeal, and it is easy to see why not. Christianity's early progress was not in that world at all, but in the Greek world, which was on a higher plane of sensibility and understanding.

more on such a subject than he does in the above quotation from xv, 44.

Suetonius, a gossipy individual, once Hadrian's private secretary, wrote his books between A.D. 98 and 138. In his *Lives of the Caesars*, "Claudius," Chapter 25, he says, "He [Claudius] banished from Rome all the Jews, who were continually making disturbances at the instigation of one Chrestus."

This is believed to be an allusion to Christ (Christus), his name being confused with the more familiar Greek and Latin name of Chrestus. From the way Christians talked of Christ's presence with them, pagans would naturally suppose Christ was living among them and causing all this excitement. Claudius' expulsion of the Jews from Rome (though Dio says he only forbade their meetings) is mentioned in Acts 18:2 as having caused Aquila and his wife Priscilla to leave Rome and move to Corinth.

Pliny the Younger in his letter to Trajan, written while Pliny was governor of Bithynia, in A.D. 112, raises the question about the Christians there, whom it seems to have been his duty to prosecute for following a non-authorized, or unlicensed, religion. Pliny inquires whether it is the "name" or the crimes attaching to the name that are to be punished. He writes the emperor that the Christians seem to be inoffensive people who gather before daybreak and sing a hymn to Christ as God, and swear not to commit crimes or wrongs. They then disperse and reassemble to eat a harmless meal together. Pliny evidently dislikes to take the extreme measures against these people that the law

A LIFE OF JESUS

CHAPTER I

Jesus' Childhood and Youth

Our first information about the lineage of Jesus is from the apostle Paul, in the opening lines of Romans, written only twenty-four or -five years after Jesus' death, where Paul speaks of him as descended from David. Of course there is not the slightest reason to doubt that he was so descended. With this statement the early gospels agree. Matthew and Luke are very explicit about it, and even Mark represents Jesus as accepting without objection and as a matter of course the salutation of Son of David, although Mark, and Matthew and Luke after him, describes Jesus as rather discounting his Davidic descent, when he said in the temple, with Psalm 110 in mind, "If David calls him lord, how can he be his son?"

But a thousand years had passed since David's prime— he reigned probably from 1013 to 973 B.C.—and almost if not quite every Jew in Palestine was probably descended from him by some line or other. Certainly it is a caricature of historical research to question an overwhelming probability, upon which the four gospels and the apostle Paul substantially agree.

Neither Paul nor Mark has occasion to speak of his

of what was so quietly and obscurely happening, and of all the help and happiness it really portended for mankind. This is why we can never outgrow Christmas. To us, it all seems understatement!

Historical research has naturally tried to make everything as easy as possible for Joseph and Mary, but that is not always the way things happen in this world, and truth is sometimes stranger than fiction. So there is really no serious argument to be brought against the twofold evidence that Jesus was born in Bethlehem, in the days of Herod the Great, probably in the last days of his reign, which ended in 4 B.C.

In Matthew's story of the virgin birth of Jesus the idea of his divine sonship is translated into narrative form. The Jewish mind instinctively cast its doctrines in the form of narrative. But while the manner of the story is clearly Jewish—the casting of dogma into narrative—the subject matter of it is just as definitely Greek; Greek legend was full of demigods—sons begotten by Zeus, with human mothers. It was a way of stating Jesus' divine sonship in terms intelligible and acceptable to the Greek mind. And to this day many people cannot think of his sonship in any other way. But while Luke takes a very similar view of his birth, our earliest sources, Mark and Paul, show no knowledge of it, and Matthew and Luke are not consistent about it, as both of them trace Jesus' ancestry through Joseph to David.

Certainly he belonged to the tribe of Judah, the one great faithful tribe, which had clung through all the cen-

to Herod Antipas as governor. He was, like Archelaus, the son of Herod and Malthace, and he ruled his district until A.D. 37. It was he who took the life of John the Baptist, and through the machinations of the Pharisees in Galilee threatened that of Jesus as well.

A third son of Herod, Herod Philip (by another wife, Cleopatra of Jerusalem), became on the death of Herod governor of a group of districts north and east of the Sea of Galilee—Batanea, Iturea, Trachonitis, and Gaulanitis— which he ruled from 4 B.C. until his death in A.D. 34. Like his father and brother he was fond of building, and rebuilt Caesarea Philippi and Bethsaida Julias into Greek cities. His wife was Salome, the daughter of Herodias.

These were the lands Jesus chiefly frequented, and the men who ruled them in his day.

Matthew says that Joseph took his family to Nazareth to live to escape the possible cruelty of Archelaus, but Luke indicates that both Mary and Joseph were residents of Nazareth before their marriage and returned there to live immediately after Jesus' birth and presentation in the temple. Mark and Paul throw no light on the problem thus created.

But Jesus grew up in Nazareth, then a town of little importance, which lies six hours' horseback ride from the present port of Haifa, and about the same distance from Tiberias and the Sea of Galilee. Nazareth was only two or three miles from Gath-Hepher, the modern El-Meshhed, where the prophet Jonah had lived eight centuries before. Over the hills to the north, three miles away, was Sep-

five books of Moses, from Genesis to Deuteronomy—the
Prophets, and the Psalms. But their prophets included the
books of Joshua, Judges, Samuel and Kings—the "Former
Prophets,"—and the "Latter Prophets"—Isaiah, Jeremiah,
Ezekiel and the scroll of the twelve Minor Prophets, as we
call them, by reason of their brevity; the whole twelve
would not bulk as large as Isaiah alone. Jesus sometimes
speaks of the scriptures as "the Law and the Prophets."
As for the book of Psalms, it was the hymnbook and the
prayer book of Jewish people. Jesus once asked his critics
whether they had never read about the stone that the
builders rejected—referring to Psalm 118.

Certainly Jesus knew the Law, the Prophets and the
Psalms. He quotes from them or alludes to them on numerous occasions, and discusses them, when called upon to do
so, with familiarity and penetration. The noble account of
marriage in Genesis, the stories of Abraham and Lot, and
Lot's wife, of David and his adventures, of Solomon and
his splendor, of the prophets Elijah and Elisha, of Isaiah
and his disappointment and his disciples, of Hosea, of
Jonah and the Ninevites, of Jeremiah's new covenant, or
agreement—it must be plain that Jesus could read the
Hebrew scriptures, and did so, with a profound understanding and appreciation of them. They have never had
such a reader!

Just how he learned to read Hebrew, for the Aramaic
translation of them was not yet written down, we can only
conjecture. But a boy as capable as Jesus could easily have
done so simply from listening closely to the weekly reading

A day was spent in the return and the search but it was not until next morning that they found him at last, in the temple, listening to the teachers as they expounded the scriptures, and asking them questions. To his mother's reproaches for the anxiety he had caused them, he only replied,

"How did you come to look for me? Did you not know that I must be at my Father's?"

They should have come to the temple first, he thought; where else in the city could he be expected to be found? For was not God his Father, and the temple his Father's house?

This idea of God must have come to him from the prophets and psalmists, and he had found it wonderfully congenial. Hosea had said they were to be sons of the living God (1:10). Jeremiah too had uttered it long before: "I have become a Father to Israel" (31:9). Malachi had said, "Have we not all one Father? Did not one God create us?" And one of the Psalmists had written, "As a father is kind to his children, so the Lord is kind to those who revere him" (103:13). David's great prayer in I Chronicles 29 begins, "Blessed art thou, O Lord God of Israel, our Father for ever and ever." Greek religious thought was coming to this great idea of God the Father of us all, as Epictetus half a century later shows, but it had long been present, though not conspicuously, in the He brew religion, in which Jesus was brought up. It is striking that he already felt this designation of God to be the most appealing and satisfying to his religious life. It was indeed

more than a new form of Pharisaism, when he encountered the strong opposition of the apostle Paul, who had been a thorough Pharisee in his youth and had seen the hollowness of it. It was this narrow attitude that made the Jerusalem church soon take a second place to the church at Antioch, which James did not control. And yet James eventually became a martyr of the new movement, being stoned to death, Josephus reports, some ten years later.

This division over religion in his home is reflected in the fact that Jesus did not find, or apparently look for, his first followers among his brothers and sisters, but among some fishermen he had met and made friends with at John's outdoor meetings down on the banks of the Jordan. Jesus evidently knew that his great new consciousness of a divine commission would find no encouragement in his own home circle in Nazareth; as he afterward said, he had come to turn a man against his father, and a daughter against her mother, and a man's enemies would be in his own household. But of course the decisive proof of this is the behavior of his mother and his brothers after he had begun to preach in and about Capernaum. They said he was out of his senses, and went up to Capernaum to try to stop him.

So Jesus' youth was probably one of dawning and increasing dissatisfaction with the prevalent form of the Jewish religion in Nazareth and in his own home. He did not in those early years see what he could do about it, but he must have felt a growing sense that there was something deeply wrong about it, which should be corrected.

terrible day of the Lord. In the boldest terms he warned the Jews who came in crowds to hear him that their descent from Abraham meant nothing to God compared with a life of helpfulness to others, with whom they must share their food and clothing. Even tax collectors, who made their living by padding their tax rolls, and soldiers, notorious as extortioners and informers, asked him what they must do. He told them bluntly that they must reform, and warned them all that someone greater than he was soon to come to institute a Messianic judgment and punish those who failed to repent and reform.

But his sternest rebuke was called forth, Matthew says, by the appearance in his wilderness audiences of people he recognized as from the dominant religious sects, the Pharisees and Sadducees. The Sadducees were dominant in and about Jerusalem, the Pharisees more generally throughout the land. Who had warned this brood of snakes, he bitingly inquired, to escape the wrath that was coming? If they were going to confess their sins and profess repentance, they had better show their sincerity in a complete change of conduct. For the descent from Abraham on which they so strongly relied counted for nothing in the sight of God. Why, he could raise up descendants for Abraham right out of the very stones that covered the ground at their feet. This was striking right at the doctrine of national religious privilege that was the cornerstone of Judaism. But the time was short; the ax was already lying at the roots of the trees, and any tree that failed to produce good fruit was going to be cut down and burned.

though the seed he sowed in his preaching along the Jordan was carried far over the ancient world. But his rite of baptism sent his followers forth not just momentarily swayed toward a better life but, in their own minds at least, publicly committed, by accepting it, to a higher course of conduct. It was the symbol of a decision reached and acted upon, a public commitment to the abandonment of old sins and the entrance upon a new life. And while John seems to have made no effort to organize his followers, it is clear that many of them organized themselves into Johannist circles out in the great centers of the Roman world, far beyond the limits of Palestine.

But what gave John's baptism everlasting significance was its effect upon Jesus. Jesus had joined the throngs of earnest, serious inquirers for the will of God who trudged off to John's meetings in the wilderness. The two men were cousins, born within a few months of each other, and probably had known each other at least slightly from boyhood. John's father Zechariah belonged to the priesthood and went up to Jerusalem once a year to take his turn in the priestly functions. But there was nothing priestly about John; his affinities were all with the prophets, and the old heroic figures of Amos, Elijah and Malachi seemed to live again in him. He revived the old prophetic view of religion as a life of uprightness in the sight of God, regardless of legalism and ritual, and enforced it with terrible pictures of judgment, wrath and punishment to come, unless men would repent and obey.

Jesus' religious life had awakened early. From boyhood

had taken possession of him. A curtain had rolled up in his mind and he saw with a new and surpassing clearness what God really wanted life to be and the great role God intended him to play in the drama of redemption. In such visions God had called Isaiah and Jeremiah to their work as prophets.

In after days he described it with his imperial imagination to his closest followers in his own unmistakable gigantesque, that inimitable quality which, Chesterton pointed out, stamps his most characteristic utterances. He saw the heavens torn open and the Spirit coming down like a dove, to take possession of him. It was doubtless the climax of much religious reflection and experience, but it was none the less the great moment, the decisive hour, not only in Jesus' life but in human experience. One man had at last been caught up as no one before into the vision of God, to be his spokesman, his Chosen, his Beloved, his Son.

This was an immensely uplifting and inspiring experience, but it was also an appalling and perplexing one. Under this new conviction, to which he had now given himself up, Jesus fled from the crowds of people that thronged about John and hurried away, driven by the Spirit, as he put it, into more solitary parts of the region for a time of reflection, as he grappled with his task and mission. After weeks of solitary wrestling that engrossed his whole mind and soul, most of the time forgetful of food and drink, he fell from his tremendous exaltation into a mood of deep depression, which he regarded as temptation.

CHAPTER III

The First Disciples

It is altogether probable that the interruption of John's work took place while Jesus was going through his solitary experience of reflection and adjustment after his great baptismal experience, with its overwhelming conviction of divine commission. Jesus returned to the scene of John's activities to find his crowds of hearers dispersed to their homes and to learn the terrible news that John himself was in prison. The opening for which he was naturally looking, to begin his own work, was thus plain before him. He went back to Galilee whence he had come a few weeks before, not, however, to his own town of Nazareth, but to the western shores of the Sea of Galilee, so densely peopled in his day that they are still strewn all the way from one end of the lake to the other with the massive remains of first-century buildings.

For Jesus had no idea of burying himself in solitude as John had done, and waiting for people to come to him. He went to them, and sought them out. The ministry of preaching into which he now threw himself carried him far and wide about Galilee and the neighboring country. Not only his method but his message was in strong contrast

So when he found John gone and his meetings broken up, Jesus turned first to the friends he had made among John's disciples, especially some Galileans who had gathered about him in the course of John's meetings.

The western shore of the Sea of Galilee was in Jesus' day a flourishing, thickly populated district, certainly all the way from Tiberias to Capernaum. Along its shores Jesus made his way northward, as an outdoor preacher, declaring that the time predicted by prophets like Daniel and Malachi had come, and the reign of God on earth, the climax of Jewish hopes, was to begin. Among the fishermen along the shore were men whom he had met before among John's hearers at the Jordan; probably he had come in search of them. He and they were not strangers to one another and he wished first to tell them of his tremendous new experience. It is striking that he does not first go home to Nazareth, to his brothers and sisters. Plainly the spiritual companionships he had formed at John's meetings he had found and still felt a closer bond than that of home. Along the shores of that beautiful lake he sought out the men he had come to know and value in the camps of John's eager listeners in the wilderness, to renew that religious fellowship and summon them to share his great enterprise.

John had preached repentance in preparation for the divine day of judgment which he believed to be imminent. But Jesus sees in God's dawning reign not a threat but a promise. Its coming is good news, which men must believe, and prepare for by repentance. This simple fact is obvious in the very word *gospel* and yet is often overshadowed by

few months to stand forth as the leader of Jesus' movement and to prove a heroic and gifted figure. He would have his moments of weakness, indeed, but his amazing personality was to carry Jesus' movement through its most trying and perilous time. It was no ordinary fisherman whom Jesus enlisted that day on the shores of Galilee. Men came afterward to think of him as the chief of the apostles.

The three men went on along the shore to where another pair of fishermen were in their boat at work on their nets, with their father Zebedee. They were James and John. They too must have been old companions of John's camp meetings, on whom Jesus felt he could rely and who had shown their attachment to him. He called them too, and, like Simon and Andrew, they had no hesitation in obeying his summons. How far it was going to carry them all, they could have had no idea. Enough that he wanted them. They were ready and glad to go with him, not stopping to ask whether it was for a day or a month; probably they did not think beyond that time. And of these four, three were to be his closest confidants, his inner circle from that moment to the end of his ministry.

From them, too, was to come to later ages the clearest picture of what he was, and what he tried to do. For it was Simon's memories of what he said and what he did in the months that followed that were to give mankind, all of us, our most intimate knowledge of him. But of that tremendous drama that was about to unfold before and around them the four fishermen could have had no idea. They were on the eve of a great experience which would

up the reign of God in the hearts of men. It was to be not a condemnation, as the prophets had thought, but an invitation, to welcome the spirit of God into their hearts and live in the assurance of his forgiveness, his care and his love—yes, and of his presence too within them.

On the Sabbath they went to the synagogue, and given an opportunity to speak, Jesus gave this as his message. It was no mere appeal to the old written Law, no effort to interpret it and enforce it, such as they were accustomed to hear from the scribes and Pharisees, but an authoritative appeal, independent of it, to a new life of harmony and fellowship with God; his spirit in their hearts, if they admitted him, would direct them and show them how to carry out his will.

This made a deep impression. But he was interrupted in his address by a loud outcry from a demoniac—a poor fellow mentally deranged and emotionally unstable who broke in upon him, crying out in fear and anger.

"What do you want of us, Jesus, you Nazarene?" He shouted. "Have you come to destroy us? I know who you are, you are God's holy One."

In Jesus' day most forms of sickness, physical or mental, were popularly dismissed as the work of demons who took possession of people. Sometimes one, sometimes seven, sometimes a whole legion of them, would take possession of a man or woman. And of course if you are sick, and everyone around you thinks you are possessed with a devil, very soon you will begin to think so too and exhibit the

out the demons. The earliest gospel is full of such incidents, and we cannot doubt that such things did happen.
When people tried to thank him, he would say,

"It is your faith that has saved you!"

With such contagious faith in the goodness and the
power of God and his own convincing good will and kindness of heart, certainly one of his leading traits, he also
roused in them the will to health and sanity and life,
always such a reinforcement and often even a necessity
to any cure.

The news of this spread rapidly through the town and
over the countryside, and right after sunset, when the
Sabbath day was over, people brought their sick and
demon-possessed to Simon's house for Jesus' aid; the whole
town seemed to have gathered at Simon's door, and again
Jesus helped and cured them. The truth is, nothing about
the early ministry of Jesus is plainer than that it was
chiefly as a wonder-worker, a benefactor and doer of good
to people in physical or mental distress that he was first
known. This gift of his impressed the simple people about
him far more than his religious message, and even dis-
tracted their minds from it—so much so that soon he felt
obliged to instruct the people he cured to say nothing
about it, but keep the fact to themselves. But that he did
such things on many occasions colors almost every page of
the earliest gospel and remains a striking evidence of his
great desire to relieve the physical as well as the moral
misery he saw about him. A great consciousness of the
needs of the people about him had come over him. His was

Gospel of Mark is the great answer to that question, as the curtain rises on the kingdom of God.

Luke is the only one of our ancient sources to give us light on how the life and work of Jesus are to be fitted into the chronology of his times. Luke says that when Jesus began his work he was about thirty years of age (3:23). If John's work began in A.D. 28-29, the fifteenth year of the reign of Tiberius (Luke 3:1), and Jesus came to hear him soon after, say in the autumn, and John's arrest took place soon after Jesus' baptism, and Jesus began to preach almost immediately after John's arrest, Jesus must have begun his work at the earliest toward the end of A.D. 28, and if he was born in 4 B.C. he would then be thirty-one or thirty-two. This would limit the time of his active ministry to little more than six months.

Many people find satisfaction in the view that Jesus was just another prophet, like one of the prophets. He certainly had much in common with them. But his unfailing devotion to helping his fellow-men, and women and children, the sick, the blind, the lame, the mad, the fearful, the miserable, of every kind, which the oldest gospel represents as his leading trait, marks him as supremely a doer of the will of God. This was no advertising campaign, to attract hearers for his message, but an irresistible overflowing of love and good will and compassion for the sheer misery of mankind, a revelation of God's own attitude, which was not vindictive and judicial but full of pity and forgiveness. This is the supreme meaning of Jesus' won-

has come, the reign of God is among you; repent and believe this good news.

For Jesus knew that its good news far outweighed its menace, of punishment and destruction. His faith in God was such, and his conviction of God's goodness and love was such, that he knew the reign of God in men's hearts on earth meant far more of happiness, usefulness and joy than of penalty and punishment. His own life was a supreme illustration of what life in the kingdom of God could be, for it was overflowing with ministries of good will and helpfulness to all about him. He lived the gospel that he taught, and men sometimes wonder which outweighed the other, his life or his teaching.

Most of us are hardly equal to our own private griefs and burdens, but Jesus boldly took upon himself the burdens of all about him. He evidently felt that it was wrong to pass by any scene of suffering that he could relieve, without relieving it. Far from using this to advertise his mission, he tried to get the people he helped to say nothing about it, but they persisted in reporting what he had done for them, and his reputation as a wonder-worker threatened to eclipse what he regarded as his real work, of preaching repentance, and the presence of the kingdom of God. Very soon he found it impossible to visit towns at all, and had to stay out in unfrequented places, where people seriously interested would seek him out and hear his preaching.

poor, releasing the prisoners, giving sight to the blind, and setting the downtrodden free.

So from the very outset of his ministry Jesus displayed that real and deep concern for the personal needs of men and women that has made him ever since the symbol of such helpfulness and sympathy. Yet this new power to attract and interest and benefit the common people about him gave Jesus no little anxiety. His host in Capernaum observed that he got up long before morning, and went off by himself to a lonely place to pray. How was he to use this rising popularity wisely and effectively? In the morning his new disciples, Simon at their head, followed him and found him, to tell him that everybody was looking for him. His fame as a wonder-worker had begun; that was why they were looking for him. They wanted to see the man who had cured them the night before, and perhaps witness further wonders from him.

From this prospect Jesus turned away, without explanation. He said to them,

"Let us go somewhere else, to the neighboring towns, so that I may preach in them too, for that is why I came out here."

He had left the house to avoid just the situation that had developed, and to be ready to move on, to tell his message in other places as he had already done in Capernaum. His preaching must have precedence over his curing the sick.

And now began that strange pilgrimage of Jesus with his faithful four, among the towns of populous, flourishing Galilee.

utterly simple and unpretending, interest the reader in
spite of himself. They are so short the reader cannot be
bored, and so vivid and varied that he is carried along. He
is seeing, as Dr. Horton put it, "the Cartoons of St. Mark."
Each might in other hands be expanded into a long narrative; of course it has been done. But no one has ever told
the stories so effectively as Mark did, following as best he
could the words of Peter, as he had heard him tell them to
his Roman audiences four or five years before.

In many of the towns Jesus visited, he or his four companions had friends or relatives with whom they could
lodge; in others his rising reputation would find entertainment for himself and his companions. As in Capernaum,
he preached in the local synagogues, for his message was
not hostile to the sound teachings of Judaism, but rein-
forced them. The great Shema, still the rallying cry of the
Jews, with its noble demand that men love God with their
whole hearts and souls and with all their might, he declared the first, the great command, and put beside it the
words of Leviticus, "You must love your neighbor as you do
yourself." He was not for a moment to be thought of as
undermining the Law and the Prophets, their great scriptures; he had come not to destroy but to fulfill and enforce
them.

But the prevalent religion of Palestine was Pharisaism,
which in its devotion to the Law had built a fence around
it, and prescribed so many trivial refinements of its precepts
as to reduce it to a huge system of minute details of conduct. The result was, the basic attitude of heart was lost in

well-to-do Jewish house. Arriving late one Friday night, without his key, he thoughtlessly pressed the button of the doorbell, and was soon admitted to the house. His employers, however, were horrified at what he had done. As the Sabbath had begun, he should not have rung the electric bell, but have knocked. On the Sabbath, he was informed, they never used electric bells, or even electric lights, resorting to candles instead. This is precisely the procedure of Pharisaism, adjusted to modern life. It clothed a host of perfectly harmless acts with what it stigmatized as disobedience to God. The result was a system so elaborate and artificial that common people who had to earn their livings could not keep up with it, and so fell outside the circle of religion. These the Jews dismissed from their minds as "people of the land." As the Pharisees put it, "These common people, who do not know the Law, are doomed!"

In this interest in such religious outcasts, as Dr. Fosdick has recently pointed out, Jesus struck a new note in religion.

For it was to these common people, scattered through the towns of Galilee, that Jesus now began to carry his message of God's love and care, and their right to think of themselves as his children. In doing so of course he disregarded and practically set aside most of the trivial and indifferent detail to which the Pharisees had reduced religion, and recalled those who heard him to a simple but deep trust in God as their Father, whom they must love beyond everything else, and to a life of love for their

CHAPTER V

The First Clash with the Pharisees
and the Choosing of the Twelve

After some time spent in thus moving about Galilee, Jesus
returned to Capernaum, which he evidently regarded as
his home and headquarters. A greater crowd than ever immediately surrounded the door, and some determined
people, who wanted his help for a paralytic friend, had to
make an opening in the flat roof of the one-story house and
lower the sick man on his mattress into Jesus' presence.
This is one of the most extraordinary and yet realistic
stories in all the record of Jesus' cures. Jesus told the poor
fellow that his sins were forgiven. In an age when sickness
and misfortune generally were regarded as divine punishment for wrongdoing, this was unexpected and blasphemous. What right had he to forgive the man's sins? Some
of the scribes, the professional champions of the Mosaic
Law, were sitting about him, listening, and these thoughts
at once occurred to them. Jesus saw what they must be
thinking, and called upon the sick man to get up, and pick
up his mat and go home. And to the amazement of everybody, Mark declares, the man obeyed.

day or soon after were doing so, apparently at Simon's house, where Jesus was now staying. Levi's joining the movement had led other men of his calling to come in to dine with them, and with them others who made no pretense of observing the rules of the Pharisees. This shocked the legal experts among the Pharisees, and they called the disciples' attention to its impropriety.

"Why does he eat with tax collectors and irreligious people?" they inquired.

When Jesus heard of it, he said to them,

"It is not well people but sick ones who have to have the doctor. I did not come to invite the pious but the irreligious."

This of course led to further criticism of Jesus by the Pharisees, for they were strongly opposed to eating with anyone who did not observe the Law with all their elaborations of it. The legalists regarded people like Levi and his friends as disreputable.

Another ground of objection soon presented itself. The pious Pharisees and even John's disciples, of whom there must have been many in Capernaum, were observing one of the Jewish fasts which were scattered through the year, in July, August, October, January and March. If the fast was for more than one day, Monday and Thursday were the days for its observance, and those who fasted were easily identified by the neglect of their personal appearance and their somber manner and expression. People were quick to observe that Jesus and his group of followers were not observing the fast days, but eating their meals and

to be an act of reaping, and unlawful on the Sabbath, when work was forbidden by the Law.

The Pharisees were quick to seize upon this trivial incident, and to tax Jesus with it. His disciples, they told him, were breaking the Sabbath law.

He reminded them of what David did when he and his men were in need of food, and took the very Presentation loaves from the altar, which no one but the priests were, under the Law, permitted to eat.

"The Sabbath," he declared, "was made for man, not man for the Sabbath." Human need, always as we have seen so important to the mind of Jesus, was paramount. He does not stop to argue about their trivial legalistics, but strikes to the heart of the institution. Why, of course it was for human need—that of rest—that the Sabbath was instituted; they have inverted its significance. The Law itself for that one day emancipated man and beast, slave and free, from labor (Deuteronomy 5:14). Man—for that is what Son of Man means here, as it does so often (more than ninety times) in Ezekiel, in Daniel 7:13 and sometimes in the Book of Enoch (46:2, 4), where it seems to be on its way to being used of the coming Messiah—man and his needs are supreme over any institution, even one as sacred and ancient as the Sabbath. Jesus frequently spoke of the Son of Man and spoke in the name of the Son of Man. While he sometimes, as here, used the expression in the ordinary Aramaic sense of man, he often used it of himself as representing mankind: "For the Son of

He held it out, and it was cured.

This dramatic rebuke of them and their position crystal-
lized the Pharisaic attitude toward him into mortal enmity,
and they got together with the Herodians, probably func-
tionaries or agents of the court of Herod Antipas, the governor of Galilee, to secure his execution, as a breaker of the
Sabbath, in accordance with Old Testament law.

News of this danger soon reached Jesus and his circle.
There were many disciples of John there, and Jesus himself now had a good many partisans in Capernaum and in
Galilee generally, so news of his danger was bound to
reach him before long. It was not at all impossible that he
would be done away with on some pretext or other, to
satisfy the local Pharisees who had now become definitely
his enemies. To execute him by stoning, for breaking the
Law, might be impossible, but their relations with Herod's
people could easily supply the means for their end. John
himself had been picked up by Herod's people—just such
Herodians—and was in prison, though his end was not far
off.

The shadow of the cross already falls across the gospel
story, though Jesus has been at work only a few weeks.

It was a very serious situation. Jesus has no mind to meet
death needlessly, in an obscure corner of Galilee, before
he has had any chance to lay his message before the Jewish
people, and he and his disciples, the five or six closest ones,
leave Capernaum for the "seashore." As Capernaum itself
was on the shore of the lake, it is clear that if he withdrew
from Capernaum it must have been for a distant part of

were Philip, Bartholomew, Matthew (probably another name for Levi), Thomas, James, son of Alpheus, Thaddeus (called Judas, son of James, in Luke 6:16), Simon the Zealot, and Judas Iscariot. The Zealots were a body of revolutionaries to which this second Simon belonged or had belonged.

That Isaiah and his tragic experience were in Jesus' mind in these early days of his work appears again soon after, when the disciples asked him about his use of parables, to which they evidently objected, and he told them the meaning of their close association with himself.

"To you," he said, "has been entrusted the secret of the reign of God. But to those outsiders everything is offered in figures, so that

" 'They may look and look and yet not see,

And listen and listen and yet not understand;

Lest possibly they should turn and be forgiven.' "

These were the bitter words which Isaiah used when his message was falling on deaf ears, and making no impression on his audiences. So not only in the choosing of an inner circle of disciples, to whom he might impart the secret of the reign of God, but also in his new method of speaking, half-veiling his meaning in this new parabolic form, he certainly had Isaiah's experience in mind, for he says so.

In a famous and dramatic passage, Isaiah showed the use and probably the purpose he intended for his band of disciples, when in a mood of disappointment, almost of desperation, he said,

Jesus gathered about him on that mountainside across the lake received some vital instruction from him before they descended the mountain and took the boat back to Capernaum. For that is what they did; Jesus and his twelve followers returned home. His plans were made, and he began to see his course opening before him; and his flight from the plotting Pharisees was only a temporary retirement from the scene. If he can keep these men about him, and teach and train them, his work will go on, even if he is taken away.

It is at this point in the story that Luke has his brief account of the sermon we know so well in Matthew as the Sermon on the Mount, a sweeping statement of the kind of life the kingdom of God demanded of its members.

It is one of the things that led Renan to say that the Gospel of Matthew was the most important book in the world. It is a tremendous formulation of the attitudes that were to prevail in the kingdom of heaven, and yet, though it set human relations on a new footing, it could all have been uttered in twenty minutes. Where else in all history was so much said in so short a time? It is the program of a new day in man's morals. This is how he is to act, in the new kingdom of heaven, the reign of God on earth, which Jesus was actually inaugurating.

The evangelist presents it in a most dramatic manner. Jesus' preaching in Galilee has been a great success. Crowds of people from other parts of Palestine—Decapolis and Judea, even Jerusalem and Trans-Jordan—follow him wherever he goes. And seeing this, he goes up on the mountain! What an extraordinary thing to do, for he can hardly hope the crowds can follow him there! Up on the mountain, he seats himself—a signal that he is about to teach, for the Jewish teacher sat, and his hearers stood. His disciples understand his action and gather about him to hear what he is going to say, and he opens his lips to teach them.

What is the meaning of this elaborate introduction, with its strange setting—on the mountain—and its almost pontifical climax: "he opened his lips to teach them"? Of course it means that what he is now about to say is of the utmost importance and value. For the reference to the mountain would recall at once to the Jewish mind another great religious teacher, who went up on the mountain—

Blessed are you when people abuse you, and persecute you,
   and falsely say everything bad of you, on my account!
Be glad and exult over it, for you will be richly rewarded in
      heaven,
   for that is the way they persecuted the prophets who went
      before you!

This vivid setting forth of the standards of happiness in
the new kingdom is, of course, basic to the presentation of
the ethics of the kingdom that follows. The ninefold
Beatitudes have no precise parallel in the Psalter, but there
is a sixfold sequence at the beginning of the Song of the
Three Children—the Benedicite—in the Apocrypha. This
striking beginning of the great sermon has also had a separate history of its own, as a beloved piece of Christian
liturgy, the Beatitudes. For Luke's set of four, followed by
four curses, in the old Hebrew manner, while powerfully
put in the second person, and in some ways of a more primitive sound than Matthew's, need not have been the only
instance of Jesus' employing this telling way of presenting
his religious ideals. Indeed, Matthew too employs the
direct form, Blessed are you, as the climax of the Beatitudes as he gives them. And obviously both series reflect
the later persecution experience of the early church (Luke
6:22, 23). So Matthew's may be thought of as an assem-
bling of such blessings, uttered at various times; the whole
sermon is probably built up from Matthew's sources into
its present proportions. As Walter Pater said, the genius
for liturgy was one of the chief endowments of the early

needless oaths, retaliation, hatred of one's enemies, ostenta-
tious praying, giving and fasting—these are wrong. We
must trust the care of God, and not go after wealth. Uprightness and character that will please him are the only
worthy goals for our efforts.

Jesus saw that religion could never be adequately set
forth as a legislation to be obeyed. The Torah was a legal
code, of crimes to be punished, not a moral standard, of
ideals to be attained. What men needed was to be kept
from anger and contempt, and calling each other vile
names, against which the Torah had nothing to say. Adul-
terous wishes and frivolous divorces are morally wrong. It
is not enough to avoid perjury; men must speak the truth.
Over against the Torah, as Whitehead says, the life of
Christ has the decisiveness of a supreme ideal.

Much is being said nowadays in praise of Pharisaism,
and it had indeed had a noble beginning, in resistance to
the compulsory assimilation to Hellenism that Antiochus
the king of Syria had tried to force upon his subjects two
centuries before. The Jewish Puritans of his day formed a
body of Separatists, who would not conform to his demands or give up their distinctive national and religious
habits of life. The triumph of their cause transformed
their position from a desperately heroic situation to one of
importance and privilege. They found themselves the custodians, as they thought, of the true religion of Israel, the
core of which was for them the Law, the Torah, the five
books of Moses. These they canonized and idolized, embel-
lishing them with elaborate interpretations, which they

placent Jew, who felt that he had fulfilled the Law, and so done all God asked of him.

But to Jesus, what God asked was something very different. It was an attitude of such indefatigable kindness to one's fellow-men that even the harsh demand of their Roman masters for enforced personal service—carrying a Roman soldier's baggage for a mile for him, if demanded— is not to be refused, or even resented, but so cheerfully performed that a second mile of service is volunteered, out of sheer good will. They must indeed be perfect, like their heavenly Father. This carried his followers out of the realm of Jewish attitudes altogether. It went beyond the Golden Rule. It was, as Dr. Colwell puts it, no "measure for measure" morality.

When they pray, they must not resort to long strings of empty phrases, like the heathen. New light has been thrown on Jesus' meaning by the Isis Litany, probably contemporary with Jesus (the Oxyrhynchus papyrus of it is of the early second century), which recites a long series of titles given to Isis in different places, as well as the functions ascribed to her; the papyrus, though only a fragment apostrophizing the goddess, takes ten minutes to read aloud. Jesus offered his disciples a prayer of the utmost brevity and simplicity, which became and remains the most valued treasure of his followers everywhere. Yet its recital takes hardly more than half a minute. *Lord's Prayer*

But to paraphrase or summarize the Sermon on the Mount is futile. It is so crisply, forcibly put that any substi-

modern world is coming to see that the remarkable thing about it is its sheer realism; nothing else will actually work.

The Sermon on the Mount *told* Jesus' hearers how to live in the kingdom of heaven; his own life of tireless usefulness *showed* them how to do it. He went about doing good. That this was the real sense the early church drew from his life is shown by the bold words of the Gospel of John, eighty years later: "Whoever believes in me will do such things as I do, and things greater yet, because I am going to the Father."

Through his sermons and parables he shows that "first-hand intuition into the nature of things" of which Whitehead speaks.

were new figures among them now. His relatives had come over from Nazareth, a day's journey away, to stop him. James, his eldest brother, was doubtless at their head, that remarkable man who after Jesus' death became the leader of Jesus' Jewish followers and the head of the church in Jerusalem, the man who did so much to make the Christian movement a new variety of Pharisaism but found a great opponent in the apostle Paul.

Not only Nazareth but faraway Jerusalem has heard about Jesus, and scribes from there have appeared to declare that he is himself possessed by Beelzebub, and that is why he can drive out demons. Jesus deals with them first.

"How can Satan drive Satan out? If Satan has rebelled against himself, and become disunited, he cannot last long, but is nearing his end. No one can go into a strong man's house and carry off his property, unless he first binds the strong man! After that, he can plunder his house."

This was really a little parable, of the kind Jesus now proposes to employ. But after it, he speaks plainly, beginning with the expression he used to emphasize his words:

"I tell you, men will be forgiven for everything, for all their sins and all the abusive things they say. But whoever reviles the holy Spirit can never be forgiven, but is guilty of an unending sin!"

He felt himself possessed with the spirit of God and he would not tolerate any disparagement of that endowment.

Then came his mother and his brothers. Joseph was probably dead by this time; certainly the silence about him

that new approach which he was to find so fruitful, and make so famous, that it has come to be actually identified with him; it was the parable. The parable is an application of fiction to moral instruction. Nathan in II Samuel 12 had used it, with the story of the poor man's ewe lamb, and Isaiah used it (Chapter 5) in the story of God's vineyard. The leading rabbis of Jesus' day also spoke in parables. But Jesus used parables so often and so effectively that many people to this day actually think he originated the parable, or monopolized it.

There was, to begin with, the immensely suggestive parable of the sower, such a warning to careless, casual listeners. It seemed to say to them, "Look out! Which kind of ground are you going to be?" It appealed at once to the familiar experiences and observation of his audiences, and entertained them as narratives generally entertain, but left in thoughtful and inquiring minds a deep religious suggestion. This was only one of the many stories he told the crowd there on the lake shore, not drawing any morals but leaving the explanation to the listeners themselves. The parable had all the attraction of a puzzle or a problem. What did he mean by it? they would inevitably ask themselves. He quickened their interest and curiosity by adding,

"Let him who has ears be sure to listen!"

There was more in the story, he wanted them to see, than met the eye, as we say; it called for close attention and reflection.

They must give full measures; if they do, they will receive full measures, and even more will be added, a paradoxical observation, yet profoundly true.

When his explanations to his disciples were concluded, he told them to cross the lake to the other side. The lake is only eight miles across but, set as it is in the mountains, it is liable to sudden storms. When they were well on their way across, one of these now swept down upon it. Jesus was lying in the stern, asleep on a cushion, when they woke him with a reproach:

"Master, does it make no difference to you that we are sinking?"

But he calmed their fears, and bade the waves subside. The wind went down, and sea was calm again. He said to them,

"Why are you afraid? Have you still no faith?"

He kept up their courage until the danger was over—always, of course, the religious approach to peril. God does not excuse us from it, but he will give us the courage to face it.

When I visited the Sea of Galilee in my student days, fifty years ago, the boats in use were sailboats some twenty-two feet long and eight feet wide, which the five native boatmen rowed when the wind failed. There were four of us in addition to the boatmen, and we were not crowded. I suppose the boats in use on the lake in Jesus' day were much the same, and it must have been in such a boat that Jesus and his disciples after the storm landed on the other side of the lake at Gerasa, probably the modern Kersa, on

right mind, a great contrast to his former condition when they had felt obliged to chain him up, and even that did not restrain him. But they were heathen, for Jews could not keep pigs, and were more concerned with the loss of their pigs than with the recovery of the demoniac. So they begged Jesus to leave their district.

Only the poor demoniac hated to see him go, and begged to be allowed to go with him. But Jesus would not permit this.

"Go home to your own people," said he, "and tell them all the Lord has done for you, and how he took pity on you." So the man went off, telling all over Decapolis—the country of the Ten Towns—what Jesus had done for him.

Jesus and his disciples now set sail for the western shore of the lake, which at this point was eight miles across; they were probably all with him on this tour of the lake, for he had just appointed them to be his companions. One such boat as I found on the lake fifty years ago would have held them all, but Mark says that other boats were with Jesus when he set out to cross the lake to Gerasa. Just where he landed on the western side is not stated. He proved to be on his way to Nazareth, and Tiberias, well down the west shore, would seem the natural point to make. But Tiberias was built on the site of a graveyard, and considered by the Jews unclean; the town is never mentioned in the New Testament. From Magdala a few miles north of Tiberias, and some six miles south of Capernaum, a well-known road led to Nazareth, a day's journey to the southwest.

But even as he spoke, people came from the synagogue leader's house to report that his daughter was dead, and that it was of no use to trouble the Master any further.

Jesus, however, disregarded them, and told the synagogue leader not to be afraid or lose his faith. Then he took Peter, James and John and leaving the others behind he hurried to the house. There the lamentation for the dead had already begun, they were so sure the child was gone. But Jesus said to them,

"What is the meaning of all this confusion and crying? The child is not dead, she is asleep."

Then turning the wailers out, he took his three disciples and the child's parents and went to her bedside, grasped her hand and said to her in Aramaic,

"Little girl, get up!"

To their utter amazement the child obeyed, got to her feet and walked. He forbade them to tell of it, but told them to give her something to eat.

But the furor these two cures must have produced, a form of popularity he had already found unfavorable to his great religious message, hastened his departure from the town, and he set off with his band of disciples for Nazareth, a walk of some seven or eight hours. The road from Magdala or any of the principal west-shore towns led through the mountains then very much as it does now, through Hattin, Lubieh, Khan et-Tujjar and Kefr Kenna to Nazareth, which was pleasantly situated on the northern slope of a basin of hills, facing toward the south. A fine spring, now known as the Virgin's Well, gave the town

Luke says that there was given him the roll of the prophet Isaiah, and that he unrolled it and found the place where it says

"The spirit of the Lord is upon me,
   For he has consecrated me to preach the good news
      to the poor,
   He has sent me to announce to the prisoners their
      release, and to the blind the recovery of their sight,
   To set the down-trodden at liberty,
   To proclaim the year of the Lord's favor!"

Then he rolled up the roll, and gave it back to the attendant, and sat down to teach. The eyes of everyone in the synagogue, Luke goes on, were fixed upon him. And he began by saying to them,

"This passage of scripture has been fulfilled, here in your hearing today!"

This was the nearest thing to an assertion of his Messianic mission that he had yet made, in public, as far as our earliest records, Mark, Matthew and Luke show. Certainly he was here identifying himself with God's Suffering Servant, of the later chapters of Isaiah.

Not long ago, on February 19, 1948, a young American scholar, Dr. John C. Trever, discovered in Jerusalem a scroll of Isaiah twenty-four feet in length, written in the second century before Christ, and so actually old enough to have been used by Jesus in the synagogue in Nazareth, in A.D. 29. We cannot, of course, for a moment claim that this is so, but it was doubtless just such a scroll of Isaiah

tion was one of astonishment and satisfaction; they were
proud of their townsman:

"Isn't he Joseph's son?" they whispered to one another.
But others said,

"Where did he get all this?"

"How does he come to have such wisdom?"

"How are such marvelous things done through him?"

"Isn't he the carpenter, Mary's son, and the brother of
James, Joseph, Judah and Simon? And aren't his sisters
living here among us?"

And when he went on to tell them that no prophet was
ever welcome in his own country, and remind them that
Elijah and Elisha did their greatest wonders outside of
Israel, they were greatly incensed and got up and hurried
him rudely out and up the hillside he knew so well to the
top of the Jebel-es-Sikh, to throw him over the precipice.
But with his awe-inspiring mien, he strode through the
midst of them and was gone.

Jesus was surprised at the failure of the people of Nazareth to show any faith in him, but he continued on his
way, teaching among the villages.

experience at his baptism, and gave them an account of his temptation experiences so immensely dramatic that no one else could possibly have expressed it. The style of Jesus was in fact one of amazing imagination and vigor. It has been characterized as "gigantesque"—and this is no exaggeration. One explorer of the gospels after another has felt this in Mark particularly. The Gospel of Mark consists for the most part of a series of pictures or incidents, situations into which Jesus comes, and which he remedies, by doing something or saying something utterly unusual. And his remarks on these occasions flash forth like a bright sword, against the background of the evangelist's narrative—vivid, trenchant and revealing. There is an entire absence of the commonplace from his remarks and his discourses. Certainly the men who wrote the gospels were quite incapable of having originated them. Even the influence of the Old Testament prophets and Psalmists on them is relatively slight.

And yet as he went about the villages of populous Galilee it was what he did rather than what he said that won him fame. Wherever he went he did people good. It is the Gospel of Mark that makes this most apparent. He was ever the Doer; the Man of Action. In fact, it was an act of his that brought about his death, for it was really his clearing the temple of its abuses that sealed his fate in Jerusalem a few months later.

It is a striking fact that so many of the doings that the early evangelists recorded about him so much resemble the kind of thing the books of Kings relate of Elijah and

the love and mercy of God welled up within him and possessed him. The reign of God meant to him the spread of this attitude to all mankind. They were not to accept any payment at all for what they did, nor take any baggage, not even a change of clothes or shoes. They were to take no money, but seek and accept the hospitality of their hearers and, as long as they stayed in a place, not to move from the house that first received them; if no one would take them in, they were to shake off the dust of their feet as a warning to them.

Matthew amplifies these instructions with lessons that reflect the experience of Christian missionaries in the next fifty years. He undertook to bring them up to date, to serve the missionary needs of his day. The twelve were not to work among the heathen or the Samaritans, but to confine their efforts to "the lost sheep of Israel's house."

The twelve went out over Galilee, calling on the people to repent, in recognition of the reign of God. They carried on Jesus' ministry of helping the afflicted. Such a campaign must have created a decided sensation among the people, and it is not strange that word of it reached Antipas himself; he doubtless had his listening posts throughout the land, and Mark declares that he had an uneasy feeling that his old enemy John must have risen from the dead, and returned to haunt him.

On the completion of their preaching tour, the twelve returned to Jesus, to report and recruit. He was probably at Capernaum, and it would seem that they must have had a fairly definite time set for the completion of their mis-

"How many loaves have you? Go and see."

They looked, and told him,

"Five, and two fish."

He at once directed them all to sit down on the fresh grass. They threw themselves down in groups, by hundreds and fifties. Then he took the five loaves and the two fish, and looked up to heaven and blessed the loaves, and broke them in pieces, and gave them to the disciples to pass to the people. He also divided the two fish among them all. And they all ate, and had enough.

Jesus' simple example of sharing all he and his disciples had with their guests must have moved those Galileans as it moves us still. They could not do less than he had done. They followed his example. The story is an evidence of his power over their hearts, a power that has been exerted millions of times, and is exerted still. After all, it is his great example that has moved the world.

Generously distributed, there was plenty for them all. There was more than enough, for they later gathered up twelve baskets of pieces of bread and fish, left by the five thousand present. The feeding of the five thousand was a sermon in action. He taught them by example, on a grand scale, and they caught the spirit of his message of mutual concern and helpfulness.

Jesus had a tremendous personal attractiveness that made men want to follow him and do as he did. He did not have to bully or abuse them. He simply showed them the way, and they gladly took it. This has been his way ever since. He has made goodness and generosity attrac

Gennesaret, the fertile plain adjacent to Capernaum, and were at once again involved in all the usual crowds and excitement Jesus' appearance occasioned. People hurried over the countryside to report his return. The sick were brought in on their mats for his attention, wherever they heard he was, and laid in the market places where he was likely to pass, so that they might just touch the tassel of his robe.

came to him when on returning to the scene of John's meetings, he had found them gone, and John himself, by the orders of Antipas, hurried off to prison. The withdrawal of John from the scene cleared the way for Jesus to begin to preach, and he set out at once for Galilee, to find his old friends of John's fellowship, with his message of repentance and welcome for the good news of the reign of God now dawning upon the world.

Once when Jesus had been praying, his disciples said to him,

"Master, teach us to pray, as John taught his disciples."

That John had taught his disciples how to pray seems to have been the occasion for Jesus' doing so for his. Luke places this incident in the course of Jesus' last journey, through Trans-Jordan to Jerusalem, while Matthew incorporates it into the collection of Jesus' sayings on the way to live in the kingdom of heaven which we call the Sermon on the Mount. Matthew's form of it is somewhat longer and more liturgical than Luke's, which is without "thy will be done," and "deliver us from evil." But in use the prayer tended to be filled out into slightly fuller proportions, as the liturgical addition of the beautiful doxology, drawn from David's prayer in I Chronicles 29:11, 12, which we all use in worship, clearly shows. The origin of the prayer is probably just what Luke describes, and Jesus himself is very likely to have used it in a variety of forms. He probably intended it more as an example of what prayer should be than as a fixed and exclusive form of prayer.

Suffering Servant of the Lord, of whom this part of Isaiah has so much to say. If he is to accept the great role of Messiah, that is the kind of Messiah he is to be.

When John's disciples were gone, Jesus went on to speak to his own followers about John. With his inimitable rhetoric he probed their motives and anticipations when months before they had flocked out to the wilderness to see John the Baptist. What did they expect to find? A weather vane? A courtier? It was a prophet that drew them out there, and more than a prophet! No other than the new Elijah, foretold in Malachi, sent to prepare the way.

"But to what," he went on, "can I compare this present age? It is like children sitting about in the bazaars, and calling out to their playmates,

" 'We have played the flute for you and you would not dance;
We have wailed and you would not beat your breasts!'

For when John came, he neither ate nor drank, and people said, 'He has a demon!' Now that the Son of Man has come, he does eat and drink, and people say, 'Look at him! A glutton and a drinker, the companion of tax collectors and irreligious people!' And yet Wisdom is vindicated by her actions!"

It is plain that Jesus feels that he is carrying out the role of the Suffering Servant of Isaiah's prophecy, not at all the traditional Jewish view of the Messiah.

It was Herod Antipas who imprisoned John, evidently

wanted. After going out to consult her mother, she came back to the banquet hall and said to the governor,

"I want you right away to give me John the Baptist's head on a platter!"

This horrible request sobered Antipas, but with all his boon companions about him he had not the courage to refuse, and he gave her what she asked. John was evidently at this time in prison at Antipas' capital, Tiberias. This daughter of Herodias is usually supposed to be the Salome who was, or became, the wife of Philip, the governor of the district northeast of the Sea of Galilee. When Philip died, five years later (A.D. 34), his domain was given to Herodias' brother Agrippa I. When in A.D. 36 Aretas destroyed the army of Antipas, Josephus says some of the Jews thought it was a punishment for Antipas' putting John to death.

A year later, after Philip's death, the willful Herodias again proved her husband's evil genius. The emperor Gaius on his accession in A.D. 37 gave what had been Philip's territory to Herodias' brother Agrippa I, with the title of king, something Antipas had never had officially, although the Gospel of Mark speaks of him as king. Herodias prevailed upon Antipas to visit Rome and ask a similar title for himself, but the new emperor exiled him to Lugdunum, the modern Lyons, instead, and Herodias decided to go with him.

religion, Genesis to Deuteronomy, purposely refrained from writing anything about religion, preferring to commit any worth-while decisions by their rabbis to memory and hand them down in that way. This was "the tradition of the elders," so often referred to in the gospels. Paul in his Pharisaic period had been fanatically devoted to what the forefathers had "handed down." In fact the Book of Enoch (from the first century before Christ), Chapter 69, expressly says that it was one of the fallen angels, Penemue, that taught men to write, "and thereby many have sinned from eternity to eternity and until this day. For men were not created for such a purpose, to give confirmation to their good faith with pen and ink"—69:9, 10. No wonder, in such an atmosphere, the decisions of the rabbis went for generations unwritten, and we may well wonder whether all of them were ever finally recorded. That is, the picture given in the late Mishnaic codification, about A.D. 200, may be expected to be far from complete, and its silence on a subject can hardly be treated as decisive evidence, over against a written record from the first century.

It is also noteworthy that in Luke's great account of the final journey through Trans-Jordan, this same practice comes up again, in a different district, and from a different source, unknown to Mark and itself unacquainted with Mark—a double attestation of the practice as in vogue on both sides of the Jordan, and in the south as well as the north. In the incident in Trans-Jordan, Luke 11:38, a Pharisee has invited Jesus to take lunch with him at his

"You give up what God has commanded, and hold fast to what men have handed down."

He went on to illustrate this attitude of theirs with a striking instance, ironically praising their skill in defeating the plain meaning of the Law by the technicalities of their tradition. The Law said a man must honor his parents, meaning of course among other things that he must support them if they needed it. But the rabbis had made a rule that if a man declared his property "Korban," that is, devoted to God, his parents could make no claim on him for their support. So while they loudly proclaimed their devotion to the Law, under the cloak of rabbinical decisions they coolly evaded its most humane provisions.

He turned from them to the people, who were always at his heels, and gave *his* decision.

"Listen to me, all of you, and understand this: Nothing that goes into a man from outside can pollute him. It is what comes out of a man that pollutes him!"

In this utterance Jesus broke not simply with the regulations of the rabbis handed down among the Pharisees, but with the Mosaic Law itself, which in Leviticus, Chapter 11, gave long lists of birds, animals and insects which a Jew must not eat.

This is perhaps the most unequivocal instance in which Jesus definitely set aside not just the traditions of the rabbis, but the express provisions of the Jewish Law. And these were rules not simply for the priesthood but for all the Jewish people. Jesus afterward pointed out to what lengths a Pharisee would go to avoid swallowing a gnat if he saw one in what he was about to drink; why, he would

this time to the shores of the Mediterranean, and the region of Tyre and Sidon. A Roman road ran directly from near Capernaum north-northwest to Tyre, perhaps thirty-five miles away in a straight line. The road ran, and still runs, by Chorazin, Safed and Giscala to Tyre, certainly two or three days' journey on foot, as Jesus and the twelve traveled. Phoenicia had been made part of the province of Syria, so that there Jesus was quite out of the dominion of Antipas and the Herodian partisans of the Pharisees. With Jesus' determined policy of confining his work to his own people, this must have been intentional on his part, and designed to avoid a violent and probably perilous clash with his enemies in Galilee, of whose power to destroy, the recent fate of John had just given terrible proof. If Antipas could be instigated against him, anything might happen.

The seriousness with which Jesus himself viewed his situation is shown by the fact that he wanted nobody to know of his presence in the vicinity of Tyre. But as usually happened, this proved impossible, and a Greek woman of the province came to him to beg him to drive a demon out of her daughter. He answered her with startling brusqueness:

"Let the children first eat all they want, for it is not right to take the children's bread and throw it to the dogs."

He meant that his work must be for his own people. But she was too much in earnest to be hurt by his language, or perhaps something in his manner told her this was not really his own attitude, for she answered,

CHAPTER XI

The Third Clash with the Pharisees

The boat had been brought across to him from his own side of the lake, and he took it, to a place called Dalmanutha, or as Matthew calls it Magadan—possibly Magdala, on the west shore of the lake. While neither of these places has been satisfactorily identified, the narrative seems to imply that he was once more in Galilee; the Pharisees immediately confronted him, demanding a sign to prove his right to teach such startling innovations as he had proposed in their last encounter.

By a sign they meant something as astonishing and convincing as the signs Moses was shown when he was called to become the deliverer and lawgiver of his people. They are related in Exodus, Chapter 4—his staff turning into a snake, and his hand turning leprous and then well again. Moses was told that, if these signs did not convince people of his divine mission, he could pour the water from the Nile on the ground, and it would turn into blood.

When Jesus swept aside the food regulations of Leviticus with a single sentence, he must, the Pharisees argued, work some such wonder as these to show his right to do it.

Jesus only sighed deeply, and refused.

God that they were resolved with the aid of their agents in Antipas' circle to destroy him.

Jesus spent some days among the villages around Caesarea Philippi, for the most part in close conference with his disciples, the faithful twelve. He questioned them closely as to what the people among whom they had gone about so widely thought about him, and in particular who they thought he was. They gave him various answers. Some, they said, thought he was John the Baptist, restored to life; others that he was Elijah, brought back, as Malachi had foretold, as the messenger of God's covenant, the forerunner of the terrible day of the Lord's judgment and vindication. Still others, they said, thought he was some other one of the old prophets, or perhaps even a new prophet altogether, in line with the old promise of Moses, in Deuteronomy 18:15.

Then he put the question to them, personally. Who did they think he was? What did they consider his role in the great drama of Israel's religion to be?

"But who do you say that I am?"

What part did they think he was to play, what place was he to take in the progress of religion? It was no mere intelligence test; he was actually consulting them. He was weighing his own future course. The peaceful, tranquil evangelization of the masses was now belligerently blocked by the Pharisees, who with their connections at court had it in their power to put him out of the way, if he went on. They had now taken the offensive in Galilee, calling upon him for a sign from heaven, if he was to teach such sub-

Isaiah 61:1. Currently, it was sometimes appropriated by leaders of revolutionary movements, designed to cast off the Roman yoke and re-establish political independence. A term so flexible was fraught with great danger to anyone who assumed it, or even accepted it, for it sounded to Roman authority like a signal for rebellion. To proclaim himself as Messiah might win Jewish attention for Jesus and his message, but it would bring down swift Roman vengeance. Before he accepted the title and made it serve his work and purpose, Jesus was careful to reinterpret it for his closest disciples, so that there would be no uncertainty in their minds about it, as applied to him. That was to be the meaning of the Transfiguration, where they later came to see him with Moses and Elijah, the great molders of their religion. It was to that order that he belonged.

Jesus now began to tell his disciples that the Son of Man, as he called himself, must go through great suffering and be rejected by the leaders of the people, and killed, though he recalled Hosea's prediction of revival and resurrection, in two or three days. This was terrible news to the hitherto hopeful and enthusiastic band. Peter saw in it signs of weakening before the great Messianic role, and began to reprove him for it. But he answered with terrible sternness,

"Get out of my sight, you Satan! You do not side with God, but with men!"

The passion in these words reveal the emotional anguish that the prospect caused him. What he needed was strength to face the fearful ordeal before him, not encour-

kingdom to that vague and distant "day of the Lord"; he proposed that men recognize God's reign here and now, and live as individuals under its sway. The kingdom of God, he said to them, is among you, or within you; in either case it is a present reality. Jesus was well aware that God's violent triumph through an apocalyptic judgment would not be the noblest triumph for God's cause; its noblest triumph would be won only through winning the hearts of men to the will of God. But of the success of that undertaking he was sure; the Son of Man would indeed come back, in his Father's glory, with the holy angels. It is his bold, imaginative way of asserting the certain triumph of the kingdom of God he was establishing among them.

As we have seen, *Son of Man* in the gospels sometimes means (as in Aramaic) simply man, as in Psalm 8:4; sometimes Jesus himself, as Ezekiel used it of himself so often—"mortal man"; and sometimes the Messianic agent of the establishment of the kingdom of God. But just when the second of these senses blends with the third it is sometimes difficult to decide.

The week that followed must have seen great searchings of heart on the part of the twelve, as they pondered on these solemn and portentous words. One afternoon Jesus took Peter, who had ventured to question the program, with James and John, who formed with him an inner confidential circle within the group, on a long walk, and led them up on a mountain to pray. There they had an extraordinary experience. As he prayed, Jesus seemed to become a supernatural being, his clothes dazzling white,

cabeus, but prophets and lawgivers. Most interestingly Jesus instructs them to say nothing of this to the other nine or anyone else, until, as Mark puts it, the Son of Man should rise from the dead. Jesus does not wish his Messiahship discussed until he has had his own opportunity at Jerusalem to show its character.

As they went down the mountain, they asked him why the scribes said Elijah had to come before the Messiah made his appearance.

"Elijah does come first," he answered, "and reforms everything, and does not the scripture say of the Son of Man that he will suffer much and be refused? Why, I tell you, not only has Elijah come, but people have treated him just as they pleased, as the scripture says about him!"

This was clearly an identification of John the Baptist with the returned Elijah. And clearly enough, Jesus' own conception of the Messiah—his "Son of Man"—here is the Suffering Servant of the Book of Isaiah, a conception that had already colored his use of Isaiah, Chapter 61, in the synagogue at Nazareth. It must be remembered, too, that Jewish Messianic thought had never taken these great chapters to refer to the Messiah. As Dr. Fosdick puts it, "The identification of Christ in the New Testament with Isaiah's Suffering Servant was a startling innovation" (*The Man from Nazareth*, p. 122).

This significant episode, with its attendant conversations, probably took place on some spur of the Hermon range, above Caesarea Philippi, where Jesus had taken temporary refuge, outside of Galilee, from the machina-

With unspeakable pathos, the man cries out,
"I have faith! Help my want of faith!"

The story is told with the convincing detail of an eye witness. I have seen just such a wretched child writhing on the ground in a village street in Palestine.

Jesus' plans are now, we must believe, formed. But he first leads the twelve back to Capernaum, and as they go through northern Galilee he again warns the disciples of what lies before him. He is to be handed over to men who will kill him, but after three days he will rise again. This hope recalls Hosea's words, 6:1, 2:

> "He smote, but he will bind us up;
>   He will revive us in two or three days;
>   He will raise us up that we may live before him."

So at last they reached home in Capernaum again. There he asked them what they had been discussing on their long walk. They would not tell, because they had been discussing which of them was the greatest. He sat down to teach, and called them before him.

"If anyone wishes to be first," he said, "he must be the last of all and the servant of all."

We do not always realize how fully Jesus himself exemplified his ideal of humility; President Ernest C. Colwell, in his *Approach to the Teaching of Jesus*, finds that "the supreme tribute to Jesus' own humility is that no one can answer the question, 'What did Jesus think of himself?'"

Almost as though anxious to change the subject, John

He went on to tell them the searching story of the Unforgiving Debtor.

Anything now in their lives that would impair their religious development must be ruthlessly pruned away; hand, foot, eye—none of these things, however precious, must be retained if it menaced their entry into life. The reference to Gehenna—the Valley of Hinnom where the refuse of Jerusalem was thrown—reflects Jeremiah's use of the phrase, and shows again how full Jesus' mind was of the great prophets. The sinister allusions to salt and fire as purifying elements show that Jesus was preparing his disciples for his next step, which might prove such a fearful test of their devotion.

his deepest hope that they would do so. But if they did not, and he must pay for his effort with his life, he would do so in a manner which should forever commemorate his great undertaking, and make his message remembered long after he was gone. He would create a memory that should be eternal. The proof of this is the historical fact that he did so! This was surely no accident.

Mark reports, and we remember that he is speaking for Peter, that Jesus left Capernaum and went into the district of Judea, and crossed the Jordan. Between Galilee and Judea lay Samaria, which Jews generally avoided, preferring to make the journey from Galilee to Jerusalem by crossing into Perea, on the east bank of the river, a part of the modern Trans-Jordan. Jesus was evidently following that route to the capital; it was the natural course for him and his disciples to take, and besides it would take them to Jerusalem along with the hordes of people on their way to the festival of the Passover. As he went, crowds of people again gathered about him, and again he taught them as he was accustomed to do.

But Trans-Jordan, like Galilee, was governed by Herod Antipas, and the Pharisees were immediately at Jesus' heels again. They had their grapevine, their channels of intercommunication, and they were ready for him. They came to him ostensibly to learn; at least to get his opinion on a divisive, much debated question: Could a man divorce his wife? Of course, the Jewish Law of Deuteronomy said plainly that he could; if she did not please him, because he had found some indecency in her, he could divorce her

commanded on the subject. They replied with the written divorce-notice provision. A man had only to draw one up, and he could divorce his wife forthwith.

Jesus handled the matter boldly. He quoted the creation story.

"It was on account of your perversity that he laid down that law for you. From the beginning of the creation, 'God made them male and female. Therefore a man must leave his father and mother and he and his wife must become one.' " And Jesus added, "And so they are no longer two, but one. Therefore what God has joined together man must not try to separate."

There is tremendous insight here into the union of husband and wife in the felicity of a true and lasting marriage. The Pharisees evidently had no more to say on the subject. But the disciples themselves were a good deal staggered by his decision, and when they reached the house where they were staying, and were by themselves, they asked him to explain.

"Anyone," he said, "who divorces his wife and marries another woman commits adultery against his former wife, and if a woman divorces her husband and marries another man, she is an adulteress!"

This was strong doctrine. It went beyond Shammai; beyond even Deuteronomy. Against them both Jesus appealed to the fundamental constitution of the marriage relation, as so nobly expressed in the creation story. He had an amazing understanding of the deep bond that

slave dealers and brought up for the slave market; Hermas, the Christian prophet of Rome, about A.D. 100, had gone through that experience.

Jesus was advancing new views of human personality, with tremendous social implications. He had said once, probably while still in Galilee,

"Beware of feeling scornful of one single little child, for I tell you that in heaven their angels have continual access to my Father in heaven!" He went on to tell them a story of a shepherd with a hundred sheep, who lost one of them, and left the ninety-nine on the hills while he went in search of it. When he found it, he was happier about it than he was about the other ninety-nine, who were safe where he had left them. So much, Jesus thought, the individual mattered. So for the wife, the child, the individual, Jesus was greatly concerned. He saw their need and their importance, and stood up for them, in a most neglectful age, and a most neglectful world, too, for it still has much to learn from him of its responsibility for all three.

It was all just a part of Jesus' great concern for human misery, not only the sick, the crippled or the mad, but the neglected, the lonely, the misunderstood. Human suffering, physical, mental, emotional, commanded his concern and help.

One of those attracted by him on his way was a rich young man, who was interested in his preaching of the kingdom of God, and came up and knelt at his feet to ask

brothers or sisters or mother or father or children or land for me and the good news but will receive now in this life a hundred times as much in homes, brothers, sisters, mothers, children, and lands—though not without persecution—and in the coming age eternal life. But many who are first now will be last then, and the last will be first."

hostile. Those sons of thunder James and John thought the villagers should be made an example of, by being consumed with fire from heaven, as Elijah consumed the soldiers sent to arrest him—II Kings 1:10, 12. Jesus merely reproved them for their fierce demand, and they went on to another village.

One day, as they were on their way, a man said to Jesus, "I will follow you wherever you go!"

Jesus answered,

"Foxes have holes, and wild birds have nests, but the Son of Man has nowhere to lay his head!" He has no home; the man must understand that. He would seem to have embarked upon the decisive stage of his enterprise, just as Luke places it; he has set his face toward Jerusalem.

To another he said,

"Follow me!"

But the man had an excuse for procrastination:

"Let me first go and bury my father"—that is, see him through his old age to the end of his days.

Jesus said to him,

"Leave the dead to bury their own dead! You must go and spread the news of the kingdom of God!" He was offering the man a higher duty even than that to his parents.

Another man said to him,

"Master, I am going to follow you, but let me first say goodbye to my people at home."

Jesus said to him,

"No one who puts his hand to the plough, and then looks back, is fitted for the kingdom of God."

that if each pair went to a different place, Jesus must have mapped out a series of thirty-six towns and villages through which he planned to pass on his journey southward. If he proposed to spend a night in each, this would involve a journey of six weeks, for his party would hardly travel on the Sabbath. That he contemplated any such prolonged tour through Samaria is improbable; he had told the twelve when he had sent them out not to visit Samaritan towns. Pursuing his own idea of working among his own people, so emphasized in Matthew, he would find them in what the gospels speak of as "Across Jordan," exactly as we now call the same region (though much enlarged) "Trans-Jordan," from the Latin Vulgate "Trans Jordanem," rather than in Samaria. Any Jews from Galilee going to the festival in his train would certainly prefer not to go through Samaria, if they did not positively refuse to do so. So his route must have been through Trans-Jordan.

The seventy-two returned to him delighted with their reception and their success. He shared their enthusiasm.

"I saw Satan fall from heaven like a flash of lightning!" he cried. He had found the key, the weapen for evil's overthrow. Joy and gratitude filled his heart and he uttered an impassioned thanksgiving:

"I thank you, Father, Lord of heaven and earth, for hiding all this from the learned and intelligent, and revealing it to children! Yes, I thank you, Father, for choosing to have it so!

"Everything has been handed over to me by my Father,

Jesus answered him with the parable of the Good Samaritan, which a modern philanthropist has declared to be the noblest and most characteristic expression of the Christian religion. The Jericho road, which lay ahead of them on their way to Jerusalem, was notorious for the robbers who infested it. A man on his way from Jerusalem to Jericho had been robbed and beaten by some of these miscreants and left half-dead on the roadside. Passers-by paid no attention to the poor man's plight, but hurried on about their business. A priest, trudging along, took the other side of the road. So did a traveling Levite. Perhaps they wanted to escape the risk of defilement in touching a possibly dead body, which would by the law of Numbers 19:11 have made them unclean, and so incapable of performing their official duties about the temple for at least a week. They were religious professionals. It was a traveling Samaritan, a member of a detested sect, that really pitied the man and looked after him, binding up his wounds and taking him to an inn where he could be nursed back to health—even providing for his subsequent care. So it was the Samaritan who showed himself the real neighbor of the wounded Jew; he knew that true humanity knows no barriers of race or creed, when one's fellow-creatures are in distress.

In a village which may have been Bethany, though that is far from likely, Jesus was entertained by a woman named Martha, who thought her sister Mary was much more interested in listening to his teaching than in helping her with the housework. But Jesus thought women were worth

[margin note: Parable of Good Samaritan]

"Ask, and what you ask will be given you. Search, and you will find what you search for. Knock, and the door will open to you."

The old charge that he drives out the demons by the aid of Beelzebub the prince of the demons, calls forth a stern rebuke. If Beelzebub is helping to cast out demons, his kingdom is collapsing beneath him. But if it is with God's help that Jesus is casting them out, then the kingdom of God has overtaken them! It has caught up with them, it has arrived.

A woman in the crowd calls down God's blessing upon his mother, but he corrects her; his mother had not encouraged him in his task.

"You might better say, 'Blessed are those who hear God's message and observe it.'"

Even in Trans-Jordan crowds gathered to hear him speak, and he warned them against demanding a sign from him. Jonah's preaching was the only sign the men of Nineveh needed to make them repent, in the Jonah story, and they will rise up in the judgment with the men of this generation and condemn them, for they repented at Jonah's preaching, but there is something greater than Jonah here. The Greek does not mean "someone greater," it is neuter, "something greater," meaning the kingdom of God.

A great deal of Jesus' teaching in Luke's Trans-Jordan section, 9:51-18:14, and 19:1-28, reminds the reader of the more familiar Sermon on the Mount, suggesting that both Matthew and Luke have had, in addition to Mark,

ples of prophetic religion under a mass of trivial technicalities.

This outspoken rebuke of both Pharisees and experts in the Law led the scribes and Pharisees to watch Jesus more closely and to try to entrap him into some even more unguarded and outspoken criticism of their views. His reference to the murder of Zechariah right in the temple itself, as given in Luke 11:51, is evidently to the incident of the stoning of Zechariah the son of Jehoiada the priest, in the court of the house of the Lord, related in II Chronicles 24:20, 21. It was the last murder recorded in their great series of historical books, from Genesis to Chronicles, as that of Abel in Genesis 4:8 was the first. Their present generation, Jesus said, would be charged with all the murders in their history, because it refused to repent and reform.

This clash with the scribes and Pharisees was quickly noised abroad and a great crowd gathered, some taking the side of the Pharisee, and some that of Jesus. Jesus pursued the subject with his disciples, assuring them that hypocrisy was futile, as the truth was inevitably destined to come out, and urging them to courageous sincerity, in whatever circumstances. Persecution might tempt them to hypocrisy, but they had better fear God rather than men. His care would not fail them; it included even the tiniest birds. They must not fear or fail to acknowledge him before men, even if brought before synagogues or magistrates to account for their views.

This serious admonition was interrupted by a voice from

what Josephus relates in *Antiquities* xviii.3. 2), perhaps in the hope that it would rouse him to indignant revolt, but he finds in it, and a similar disaster at Siloam, only a fresh call for repentance. He goes on his way curing the sick and uttering new parables—the Unfruitful Fig Tree, the Tiny Mustard Seed, the Yeast That Raised the Dough.

Not all the Pharisees, at least in Trans-Jordan, were hostile to Jesus; some of them even warned him of his peril. Someone had asked him whether only a few would be saved, a question much discussed among the Jews, as in II Esdras 8:1-3, and he replied with the parable of the late-comers reaching their host's house too late to be admitted. The door is narrow, and men cannot take their own time about entering it. The Jews who thought themselves sure of admittance would see people from the east and west and north and south taking their places side by side with Abraham, Isaac and Jacob and all the prophets, in the kingdom of God, while they were put outside.

"There are those now last," he concluded, "who will then be first, and there are those now first who will be last!"

Just then, Luke goes on, some Pharisees came up, and said to him,

"Go! Get away from here, for Herod wants to kill you!"

Mark has shown that the Pharisees were in touch with Herod's agents up in Galilee, and now in Trans-Jordan Jesus was still in the territory of Herod Antipas.

It was probably from their Pharisaic connections that these men knew what they did of Jesus' danger, but they understood Jesus better, and were conscious of a basic

The difficulty of many of the sayings given in this section of Luke as uttered on the way through Trans-Jordan to Jerusalem is strong evidence of their genuineness, as preserving the words of Jesus. His great concern for the individual comes out strikingly in the parables of the Lost Sheep (the Ninety and Nine), and the Lost Coin. But even these fall into the background before the great story of the Prodigal Son, which is preserved only in Luke, and in this narrative of the journey through Trans-Jordan. It is followed by the startling story of the Dishonest Manager, who was threatened with discharge and took the opportunity to settle with his master's debtors on terms very favorable to them, in the hope of getting business opportunities from them after his approaching discharge. So they were to use their ill-gotten wealth to make friends for themselves in another world.

The story of the Rich Man and Lazarus follows, and then the short, moving one of the Pharisee and the Tax Collector. The Pharisee's prayer was full of complacency; he was glad of his superiority, and his virtue. But the tax collector stood at a distance, and would not even raise his eyes to heaven, but struck his breast and said,

"O God, have mercy on a sinner like me!"

Jesus said it was he that went back to his house with God's approval, and not the other, because everyone who exalted himself would be humbled, but the man who humbled himself would be exalted.

These three short stories, the Good Samaritan, the Prodigal Son and the Pharisee and the Tax Collector, are

Luke 10:21, 22, when he turned to his disciples and said, "Blessed are the eyes that see what you see! For I tell you, many prophets and kings have wished to see what you see, and could not see it, and to hear what you hear, and could not hear it!"

"Master," they said, "we want you to do for us whatever we ask."

"What do you want me to do for you?" he asked.

They said to him,

"Let us sit one at your right hand and one at your left, in your triumph."

This was a startling demand, and its effect upon the other apostles may be imagined. And especially, where did it leave Peter, their leading spirit? The sons of Zebedee certainly thought well of themselves, and proposed to make the most of the great movement in which they felt themselves caught up. They had been almost the first disciples Jesus had called. And if they demanded much of the new movement, they were prepared to give all they had to give to it. But as yet they were looking upon it as preferment and fortune.

Jesus, on the other hand, was facing a dark and perilous prospect. He said to them,

"You do not know what you are asking for! Can you drink what I am drinking, or undergo the baptism I am undergoing?"

He was going through an agonizing experience, as he had tried to make them all see, and facing he knew not what consequences, and his answer must have sobered them, but they did not hesitate.

"Yes, we can," they answered.

He must have looked at them with compassion, for he said,

"Then you shall drink what I am drinking, and undergo the baptism that I am undergoing; but as for sitting

rect road that paralleled the river but by the higher one
that ran by way of Gilead through more settled country.
Jesus kept his own counsel, but it must have been now
that he was making the private arrangements that were
afterward to bear fruit when he reached Jerusalem, and
still later when he needed a room, in accordance with the
Law, within the city in which to eat the Passover. It is
significant that he felt these arrangements must be secretly
made, such was his sense of the peril that would hang over
him at the capital. This might have been arranged after he
was settled in the village of Bethany, half an hour out of
Jerusalem, though that too must have been arranged for
during this journey, for all the accommodations about the
city would be taken by the time his party arrived there.
But certainly the provision for an ass's colt, exactly such as
Zechariah had predicted the Messiah would some day
enter the city on, to be ready at the moment Jesus planned
to reach Jerusalem, surrounded by throngs of pilgrims to
the Passover, must have been made during this journey
through Trans-Jordan; that could not wait until his ar-
rival. But Jesus clearly attached much importance to its
readiness. He is not going up to Jerusalem like a lamb to
the slaughter. He is making every effort beforehand to
dramatize his entry into the city and make it the keynote
of his great campaign there. The fact that he was coming
with only a few dozen disciples at his back, together with a
few women, only heightens the drama. Not only is he
hoping and striving to succeed; he has a course of action
in view to be followed in case of failure, that will he hopes

village they would find a colt that had never been ridden, tied. They were to untie it and bring it back to him. He went on,

"And if anybody says to you, 'Why are you doing that?' say, 'The Master needs it, and will send it back here directly.' "

Zechariah had long before predicted that the Messiah would enter the city "humble, and riding upon an ass, even upon a colt the foal of an ass" (Zechariah 9:9); the prophet called upon Jerusalem to welcome him with acclamation. It was with this prophecy in mind that Jesus had evidently taken measures while coming through Trans-Jordan, or while at Jericho, to have this animal in readiness for his use. The men in charge of the ass have their instructions, and his messengers have the expected answer. And all this is of great significance, for it means that in the Triumphal Entry into Jerusalem Jesus definitely assumed the role of the Messiah. That was what he had carefully planned. Where a man of the Western world would have stood up before an audience and said he was the Messiah, Jesus, in this highly Oriental fashion, even more unequivocally declared himself to be he, by riding into the city exactly as the prophet had foretold. It was his way of focusing attention upon himself and what he had to say to his nation, in his and their great crisis. It was no mere incident; it was a carefully planned declaration, for an immediate practical purpose. He is not simply fulfilling the prophecy; what is far more important for the biographer, he is doing it intentionally and on purpose.

from the city, when Jesus mounted; it is only half an hour's walk from Bethany to Jerusalem.

So Jesus came to Jerusalem. By what gate he entered it, and found his way through its narrow crooked streets to the temple, we cannot say. The temple he visited has utterly disappeared; we can only trace some of its substructures under the pavement of the Haram area that forms the great courtyard of the Mosque of Omar, standing over the bare rock which was the threshing floor of Araunah the Jebusite and on which stood the high altar, the altar of burnt offering of Herod's temple. This splendid piece of Greek architecture, even then not quite finished, with its dazzling marbles and noble proportions filled the ordinary Jewish heart with pride.

Jesus looked it all over; he could pass through the Court of the Gentiles into the Court of the Women and beyond that into the Court of the Men of Israel. Beyond that lay the Court of the Priests, which he could not enter, and beyond that the curtain-covered holy place and sanctuary, the innermost shrine of the Jewish religion. The hour was late; it was a long walk from Jericho to Jerusalem, and the temple courts were beginning to be deserted. Jesus surveyed it all, no doubt planning what his course should be when he returned next morning. Then he and his disciples left the temple and the city and crossing the bed of the Kidron skirted the Mount of Olives, which rises two hundred feet above the city, and made their way to the security of Bethany, on its eastern slope, where they were to spend the nights.

changing the pilgrims' Roman money into the sacred currency the temple would accept. Here were also the sellers of the doves for sacrifice, as described in Leviticus 1:14. Jesus overturned the tables, and the dove-sellers' seats. As in the court of the Great Mosque in Damascus in modern times, porters carrying goods would make a short cut through the temple, and these Jesus ordered stopped. To the crowd that these high-handed proceedings attracted, he quoted the great oracle from the book of Isaiah,

"My house shall be called a house of prayer for all the nations," and yet if the Gentiles came there to pray, they would find their part of it full of petty business, in full swing. Instead of a house of prayer they had made it, as Jeremiah put it (7:11), a robbers' cave.

This was a bold attack in the name of religion upon the privileges and monopolies of the Sadducees, who occupied the priesthood and controlled the whole machinery of temple sacrifices and offerings. That was their monopoly, and they exploited it fully. In invading the Court of the Gentiles and interfering with the business done there, Jesus was making a frontal attack on the established order in Jerusalem and making a bold bid for a public hearing for his message.

He had begun his attack by his triumphal entry, thus announcing himself as a divinely commissioned leader; he continues it by this bold interference with established custom in temple—steps calculated to capture the attention of the Jewish public and the temple authorities. Jesus is seeking a decision, at Jerusalem. And he is doing it in

been high priest for a short time not long before the appointment of Caiaphas, and still retained much of his previous influence and authority. These two are the "high priests" of the period, though perhaps other surviving ex-high priests are also meant in the gospels by the plural "high priests."

For more than two hundred years the Sadducees had been influential in Jewish religious life, and in Jesus' day they included the powerful priests and aristocrats—in short, the wealth and influence of Judea. They accepted only the Law of Moses as scripture, and rejected the Pharisaic doctrines of resurrection, together with the existence of angels and spirits. They had commercialized the temple worship, as indeed all temple worships were in that day commercialized, and conducted the worship of Judaism in ways acceptable to their Roman masters. To the religious condition of the people scattered through the country they gave little heed, demanding only that they steadily support the feasts and sacrifices at Jerusalem. The Pharisees were thus of little importance in Jerusalem, but they had their scribes there, and they participated in the deliberations of the Sanhedrin, the religious governing body of the Jews. But Jesus had already incurred the hostility of the Pharisees up in Galilee, and scribes from Jerusalem had been called in to examine into his proceedings. And now the Pharisees are more than ready to cooperate with the Sadducees in resenting what he did. They had long wanted to put an end to him and, with the cooperation of the Sadducees, began to see their desired goal

of all Palestine wandered about it with mingled awe and gratification. They felt it was Judaism's answer to the huge heathen structures, the temple of Artemis in Ephesus, the Serapeum in Alexandria, and the Capitol in Rome, the last two then the greatest buildings in the world.

It was in such a setting that a deputation of high priests, scribes and elders confronted Jesus, and boldly challenged his right to upset their established arrangements of money-changers and dove-sellers. It was not his teaching but his acts that they demanded an explanation of.

"What authority have you for doing as you do? And who gave you a right to do as you are doing?"

It was Jesus the man of action that had roused them, and brought this striking combination of Jewish authority together to confront him. For the scribes were a Pharisaic order, and the elders were members of the Sanhedrin, the council of seventy-one members, appointed from the leading priests, heads of prominent Sadducean families, and eminent Pharisaic scholars, or scribes, who formed the final court of appeal in Jewish matters in Judea. It was therefore a semiofficial body that now approached Jesus in his walk about the temple, and demanded his credentials.

He answered them without hesitation.

"Let me ask you one question, and if you answer me, I will tell you what authority I have for doing as I do. Was John's baptism from heaven, or from men? Answer me."

This question did not merely turn the tables upon them, it struck at the basis of their own inquiry. For his authority and John's came from the same source, the will of God.

they killed; and so with many others, some they beat and some they killed.

"He still had one left to send; a dearly loved son. He sent him to them last of all, thinking, 'They will respect my son!' But the tenants said to one another, 'This is his heir! Come on, let us kill him, and the property will belong to us!' So they took him and killed him, and threw his body outside of the vineyard.

"What will the owner of the vineyard do? He will come back and put the tenants to death, and give the vineyard to others. Did you never read this passage of scripture—

> "That stone which the builders rejected
> Has become the corner-stone;
> This came from the Lord,
> And seems marvelous to us?"

The bearing of the parable's picture of the treatment the Jewish people had so often given their prophets was unmistakable, and its application to the attitude the temple authorities were taking toward him was only too apparent. The delegation wanted to arrest him, for they knew the illustration was aimed at them, but he was too strong with the people for them to risk it, and while the people might not have been able to protect him, the riot they would have made might have very unfavorable results with the Roman authorities, on whom the high priest depended for the tenure of his office. They withdrew from the attack, to plan some other stratagem.

The next group to try to entrap Jesus into confusion or blunders consisted of Pharisees and their Galilean allies the Herodians, or agents of Herod Antipas. They raised a well-worn question, that of paying tribute to the Roman emperor, which it was hardly possible to answer without giving serious offense to some important group in Judaism. The Zealots considered it wrong to pay it; the Pharisees, who cared only for their religious liberties, regarded it with indifference. The Pharisees approached him with apparent approval:

"Master, we know that you tell the truth regardless of the consequences, for you are not guided by personal considerations but teach the way of God with sincerity. Is it right to pay the poll tax to the emperor or not? Should we pay it, or refuse to pay it?"

Jesus detected their design, and said to them,

"Why do you put me to such a test? Bring me a denarius to look at."

They brought him one, a small silver coin about the size of our ten-cent piece, bearing on its face the profile portrait of the reigning emperor Tiberius, almost encircled by his name and title "Tiberius Caesar, son of the deified Augustus, (himself) Augustus." Jesus had seen many such coins, but for his own purpose he asked the men who brought it to him,

"Whose head and title is this?"

They told him,

"The emperor's."

little of Sarah and her seven husbands in the Book of Tobit, which may have suggested it to the Sadducees.

Jesus replied that when people rise, there is no marrying or being married, but they live as the angels do in heaven, and reminded them of what God said to Moses in a famous passage in what we know as Exodus, "I am the God of Abraham, the God of Isaac, and the God of Jacob," clearly implying that he was still their God when he spoke to Moses, centuries after they had died, and that the relation of trust and dependence that had existed between them and God had not been interrupted by death. God, he said, was not the God of dead men, but of living. The story is also very significant as it shows Jesus' own belief in the future life. Jesus saw that the idea of the future life was involved in the soul's relation to God. If we can have communion with him, and come to trust and love him, we have entered upon a spiritual relationship which death cannot destroy. Modern Jewish scholars dismiss this argument as fanciful but it is far from being that. As St. Augustine said, probably quoting the second-century Odes of Solomon, "Join yourself to the eternal God, and you will be eternal."

In both these encounters, that with the Pharisees and that with the Sadducees, Jesus' answers had leaned toward the Pharisees' side, as compared with the Sadducees, and one of the scribes of the Pharisees felt that he was answering them well. So, not to test him, but with a sincere interest in his view of a vexed question, he put one to him.

"Which is the first of all the commands?"

and religious leadership might have opened before them! The prophets had hoped for such a day.

Jesus was pleased at the scribe's response. He saw that the man had answered thoughtfully, and he said to him, "You are not far from the kingdom of God!"

It may not be without significance that Jesus in the gospels in quoting this classic item in Jewish liturgy invariably introduces the word "mind" or "understanding" into the series, as a fourth instrument for loving God. Jewish translators of the Hebrew (Deuteronomy 6:5) render "with all thy heart and with all thy soul and with all thy might," but Jesus' form of the command, as given in Matthew 22:37 reads "mind" for might, while Mark 12:30 and Luke 10:27, though in different orders, add "your whole mind." The scribe in agreeing with Jesus repeats the command after him, "with one's whole heart, one's whole understanding, and one's whole strength," and some modern Christian scholars translate Deuteronomy 6:5 "with all your mind, and all your heart and all your strength." But Dr. R. H. Charles, the scholarly archdeacon of Westminster, felt that Jesus had here made a positive and important advance upon the ancient form of the great command, adding intelligence to the great demand for zeal of the ancient Hebrew. In loving God, one did not need to close one's mind! Quite the opposite.

No one asked him any more questions, and he raised one himself.

"How can the scribes say that the Christ is a son of

jects. Yet notwithstanding this incident in the temple, which Matthew, Mark and Luke record, there are numerous cases where he is hailed as "Son of David" by enthusiastic groups or people in need of his help, and he had not refused the title. The genealogy at the beginning of Matthew by its title designates him as descended from David, and the genealogy there and the very different one in the third chapter of Luke trace his descent through David. A thousand years had passed since David's prime, and almost every Jew in Palestine must have had some Davidic blood; Jesus could hardly have escaped it. It must be clear that what he is here denying is not his own physical descent from David, but the use of that expression as an adequate description of the Messiah, who is far more than that title conveys. He is now definitely concerned to divest the title of its political color, which was not only misleading but dangerous, and bring out its loftier religious meaning, as the one to which the Psalm in question, messianically understood, really pointed.

The people who thronged the temple courts liked to hear him, and he took occasion to warn them against the pretensions of the Pharisees, their self-constituted religious leaders throughout the land.

"Beware of the scribes who like to go about in long robes, and to be saluted with respect in public places, and to have the front seats in the synagogues and the best places at dinners—men that eat up widows' houses, and to cover it up make long prayers! They will get a far heavier sentence!"

for whoever exalts himself will be humbled, and whoever humbles himself will be exalted.

A deeper fault with Pharisaism lay in the fact that its refinements of the Law, devised to protect it from any possible violation, had hedged it about with such frivolous detail that the poor and ignorant people of the land could not observe it, and were by that very fact cut off from the comfort and support of religion. Pharisaism had made religion an aristocratic privilege. We shall find Jesus returning to this matter in the last and greatest of his parables, the Last Judgment. They were locking the doors of the kingdom of heaven in men's faces; they would neither go in themselves nor let those go in that wanted to do so. They were infinitely scrupulous about tithing, computing the required tenth upon the very smallest articles of food, the flavorings and extracts used in cooking, for fear they might unwittingly break the law, yet they left undone the far greater matters, justice, mercy and faith. Why, as we have seen, a Pharisee spying a gnat in his drink would go to all the trouble of straining whatever was in his cup, to avoid breaking the law of Leviticus 11:23, 43 against eating the tiniest winged insect, and yet go out and, in comparison, swallow a camel!

Another fatal flaw in Pharisaism as Jesus saw it was its externalizing of religion. It was all so detailed and defined that one's attention was absorbed in externals, the outside of the dish, and the heart and essence of the religious life, the attitude of spirit, was forgotten and neglected. But that was what mattered most; in fact, it was everything

the gift of a poor woman, evidently a widow, who shyly dropped two little copper coins into the mouth of one of the receptacles. Jesus was near enough to see the smallness of her contribution, and felt the relative greatness of her sacrifice. He called his disciples to him and said to them,

"I tell you, this poor widow has put in more than all these others who have been putting money into the treasury! For they gave of what they had to spare, but she in her want has put in everything she possessed—all she had to live on!"

These four verses about the Widow's Mite form the longest passage in Mark that does not reappear in Matthew, and for the obvious reason that Matthew makes so much of Jesus' denunciation of public giving that his praise of the woman's public act probably seemed to the evangelist out of line with his great hyperbole that when you give to charity you must not let your left hand know what your right hand is doing.

As they left the temple that afternoon, one of the disciples, overwhelmed with the massive splendor of the great fabric, said to him,

"Look, Master! What wonderful stones and buildings!"

He might well exclaim, no matter how many times he may have seen them before. Much of the east side of the foundation wall is still there to awe the modern visitor, with blocks of stone two and a half feet thick and twenty-six, sometimes twenty-seven and a half, feet long, perhaps hewn and put in place in the days of Solomon. Above them rose the colonnade that surrounded the great court,

living closer to actual apocalyptic realization than people
have ever lived before, if by apocalyptic is meant the end
of our world and of human life as we know it.

To Jesus it may well have seemed that Roman and Jewish currents were moving toward inevitable catastrophe.
The Zealots and nationalistic revolutionaries on the one
side, and the ruthless and rigid policies of the Roman
empire on the other, with callous and unprincipled Roman
governors and Jewish high priests to spark the explosion,
promised eventual disaster for city and nation, unless the
kingdom of heaven should win such support that his people would turn to living as men belonging to another
world. But his experience in Jerusalem has made him feel
that this is not to be, and the explosion of which he has
seen so many signs about him must occur. Peering into the
future, he envisaged strange shapes of things to come.
Nation would rise against nation, and kingdom against
kingdom; there would be earthquakes here and there, there
would be famines. These would be only the beginnings of
the sufferings. But when they saw these things happening,
they might know that the Son of Man was at hand.

A sense of great immediacy possessed him. "I tell you,"
he went on, "these things will all happen before the present age passes away. Earth and sky will pass away, but my
words will never pass away. But about that day or hour
no one knows, not even the angels in heaven, nor the Son,
only the Father. You must look out and be on the alert,
for you do not know when it will be time; just as a man
when he leaves home to go on a journey, and puts his

other direction, and it was he who carried this Hebrew genius of expression to its greatest heights. And nowhere more than in his apocalyptic pictures of the Messianic future. But as a matter of fact, this was the basis of the whole apocalyptic language, which Western minds took far too literally, and was in every case highly figurative, being one of the ways Hebrew religious teachers took to gain contemporary human attention. There is no doubt that more matter-of-fact minds unfamiliar with Oriental modes of speech have created difficulties for themselves in trying to interpret literally the apocalyptic school, and Jesus, who used so much of its vocabulary, and indeed gave it its highest expression.

In those momentous hours on the Mount of Olives, as Jesus sat talking to his disciples, as Matthew records it, his teaching in parables reached its climax in a series of three stories.

"The kingdom of heaven," he began, "will be like ten bridesmaids, who took their lamps and went out to meet the bridegroom." Everyone remembers the inimitable story. Five were wise, and took extra oil for the tiny lamps they carried, but five were foolish and did not. Everyone knows their sad story; they were shut out of the wedding banquet.

Another is the parable of the talents, the story of a man who entrusted large sums of money to his slaves, five thousand dollars to one, two thousand to another and one thousand to a third. The first and second went immediately to

part of the population, the "people of the land," who could not begin to keep up with the requirements the Pharisees had set up for religion. They had definitely refused to do it for those who were least, and this Jesus recognized as the one thing that was unpardonable in the custodians of religion.

came in with an alabaster flask of expensive perfume, and breaking it poured the perfume upon his head. Anointing the head of a guest with fragrant oil was a part of Hebrew courtesy—

> "Thou anointest my head with oil,
> My cup runneth over"—

though it was really the part of the host to provide such attentions (Luke 7:46). Some of the other guests, who were mostly his disciples, and poor men, were indignant at such extravagance. They exclaimed that it was wasteful, for the perfume might have been sold for a large sum of money and the money given to the poor. They loudly condemned the woman for wasting it.

Jesus, however, stood up for her. He saw in her action its emotional value; it showed how much she thought of him and his work. It was probably the most valuable thing she possessed, and she had lavished it upon giving him a moment's pleasure and doing him honor. Thoughts of his own great peril too colored his attitude.

"Let her alone," he told them. "Why do you bother her? It is a fine thing that she has done to me. You always have the poor among you, and whenever you please you can do for them, but you will not always have me. She has done all she could; she has perfumed my body in preparation for my burial!" The prospect of his early death had never been far from his thoughts, from the time he left Galilee for the journey to the festival. Now he went on to say,

"I tell you, wherever the good news is preached all over

Meantime Judas felt that the time had come for him to act. What can have animated him, whether he had always been a traitor at heart, looking for a chance to make something for himself out of Jesus' friendship, or whether he had a mad confidence that an actual attack upon Jesus would force his hand and stir him to some supernatural demonstration that would put him and his apostles in control of things, we cannot say. At any rate he got in touch with the high priests, and undertook to betray Jesus' whereabouts to them at a given time, so that they could seize him with nobody about to interfere. Perhaps the incident at Simon's house in Bethany precipitated his action. From this point on, at any rate, he was watching for his chance.

Jesus was very anxious to eat the Passover supper with his disciples, and on Thursday morning, when his disciples asked him where he wished them to make their preparations for it, he told two of them—Luke says Peter and John —to go into Jerusalem, where they would meet a man carrying a pitcher of water. They should follow him, and in the house that he entered they should say to the man of the house,

"The Master says, where is my room, where I can eat the Passover supper with my disciples?"

The man would show them a large room upstairs, furnished and ready, and in it the disciples were to make the necessary preparations.

It is clear that Jesus had made these arrangements in advance, even to the finding of the house by following the man with the pitcher, just as he had prearranged to have

understand the meaning to be that. As the creation story shows, the Jews counted evening and morning as making the day, so what we call the evening of the thirteenth they would call the evening of the fourteenth, their "day" running from sunset to sunset. But Mark is writing for Greeks who knew nothing of these quaint ways of speech, and found them as difficult as we do.

The festival of Unleavened Bread, a sort of Hebrew spring housecleaning festival, ushered in by the Passover sacrifice and supper, began in what we would call the evening of the thirteenth of Nisan, but the Jews called the fourteenth and counted as the first day of the festival. The disciples went into the city, found the man with the water pitcher, as Jesus had described him, and followed him to the house where the man of the house, evidently communicated with before by Jesus, received them and provided what they needed for the supper.

The usual Passover supper was punctuated with the four cups of red wine and water, the first of which was first blessed and then drunk or tasted. Then they all washed their hands (they ate of course with their fingers) and a prayer was offered, or repeated. The second cup was then drunk, and the origin of the festival was explained by the head of the household. The first part of the "Hallel" ("Praise!"), Psalms 113 and 114, was then sung. The food consisted of the roasted lamb and the unleavened bread, not a loaf to slice, as with us, but a smaller, flattish cake of bread, which would be broken with the fingers. A sauce of dates, raisins and vinegar was probably at hand in a dish,

insured their absolute loyalty, but he goes on to say it is to
be one who is dipping his morsel of bread or vegetables in
the same dish with him, meaning no doubt the dish of
sauce that served the whole table.

"It is one of the twelve, who is dipping his bread in the
same dish with me. For the Son of Man is indeed to go
away as the scriptures say of him, but alas for the man by
whom the Son of Man is betrayed! It would have been
better for that man if he had never been born!"

With this terrible warning he sought to restrain any of
them who might be planning to betray him. The scripture
referred to was Isaiah's prophecy about the Suffering Servant of Jehovah (Isaiah 53). Isaiah's pictures had been in
Jesus' mind certainly ever since his reading of Isaiah 61 in
the synagogue at Nazareth.

As the supper progressed, he took one of the round cakes
of bread, and gave thanks over it, then breaking it in pieces
he passed them around among them.

"Take this," he said. "It is my body, which takes your
place. Do this in memory of me!"

In these solemn words he was clearly taking leave of
them and of this world. He was also commanding them
henceforth to make this supper a memorial to him, which
should perpetuate his memory and his message. We now
begin to understand why he had been so much concerned
to live to celebrate the Passover with them, and why he
had taken such precautions so that nothing might interfere
with his plan, and why he had shown such great relief
when they all sat down to supper. He proposed to make

believers ate this bread and drank from this cup they proclaimed Jesus' death. It is very probable that Paul's knowledge of these events was drawn from the oral gospel of the
primitive church, to which he occasionally refers and
which had nothing to do with our written gospels or their
immediate sources.

After they had all drunk from the final cup of the Passover supper, and he had told them what it would mean to
them in after years, they sang the usual hymn, the second
part of the Hallel, Psalms 115 to 118, beginning,

> "Not unto us, O Lord, not unto us,
>   But to thy name give honor,"

and ending,

> "Give thanks to the Lord, for he is good,
>   For his kindness is everlasting."

Then they left the upper room, and found their way
down the street to the gates and out of the city. But Jesus
had had his wish, to eat that Passover with his closest,
chosen friends, and he had done it in such a way as to
stamp some things indelibly upon their memories. For now
whatever happened to him, and he felt his danger was
very near and very great, the Passover would always remind them, and all his followers after them, of him and
his sacrifice, as he now knew it to be. Paul, who wrote his
account of it, quite incidentally, in his first letter to the
Corinthians only twenty-five years after, already understood that he had said to them, of eating the bread, "Do

CHAPTER XVII

Gethsemane and the Trial

From the upstairs room in Jerusalem they went out of the city and up the Mount of Olives, on their way home to Bethany. Jesus was still downcast and apprehensive. He talked to them as they went.

"You will all desert me," he said. "For the scriptures say, 'I will strike the shepherd, and the sheep will be scattered.' But after I am raised to life again I will go back to Galilee before you."

It was evident that he was now convinced that his death was very near, but, as Hosea had said, God would raise him up, to rejoin them at some rendezvous in Galilee. Peter, however, stoutly demurred.

"Even if they all desert you," said he boldly, "I will not!"

But Jesus said to him,

"I tell you, this very night, before the cock crows twice, you yourself will disown me three times!"

But he persisted vehemently,

"If I have to die with you, I will never disown you!"

All of them said the same thing; they would never disown him.

It was a mild spring night, with a full moon, and Jesus

wanted them awake, either as sentries or as possible company in his extremity.

"Simon," he called, "are you asleep? Weren't you able to watch for one hour? You must all watch, and pray that *you* may not be subjected to trial!" And yet he knew how tired they were, and added,

"One's spirit is eager, but human nature is weak."

Again he left them and returned to his painful vigil, praying again in the same words. He was gone some time, for when he came back to them they were all asleep again, for they simply could not keep their eyes open. Again he charged them to keep awake and watch, for he knew what a risk he was taking; this was the first night he had been out of doors, near the city, instead of safe in crowded Bethany. They did not know what to say to him.

When he came back to them the third time, he said to them,

"Are you still sleeping and taking your rest? Enough of this! The time is up! See, the Son of Man is betrayed into the hands of wicked men. Get up, let us be going! Look, here comes my betrayer!"

For just at that moment, while he was speaking, Judas came up with a crowd of men with swords and clubs, from the temple authorities, to arrest him.

We must not hastily blame the Jewish people for what ensued; a great many of them were really on his side, if they could have been fairly counted. It was the dominant crowd, the Rome-appointed high priest and his agents who controlled Jerusalem, who now went into action. (Pilate's

after day in the temple, teaching, and you never seized me. But let the scriptures be fulfilled!"

He was alluding to the words in Isaiah (53:6-9 and 12) about the Suffering Servant of Jehovah, with whom, as we have seen, he had before identified himself:

> "When he was oppressed, he humbled himself,
> And opened not his mouth;
> Like a sheep that is led to the slaughter, . . .
> He opened not his mouth."

In the confusion that followed, the disciples made their escape, though Peter put in an appearance in the courtyard of the high priest's house later in the night. The high priest's crew tried to hold everybody they could lay their hands on. The story in Mark of a young man with just a linen cloth around him, who only escaped by slipping out of it when the posse tried to hold him, is told to show that they were picking up everybody found near Jesus. There is a similar incident in the Greek papyri of a man's escaping arrest by the very same device.

So Jesus was left alone with his captors, who took him down across the Kidron into the sleeping city, to the house of Caiaphas the high priest. The high priest's palace was probably located in the southwestern quarter of the city, and the houses of the priestly aristocracy were in the same general neighborhood, so that they could be readily reached, although it must have been in the small hours after midnight.

The high priest and his household were roused from

"Have you no answer to make? What about their evidence against you?"

Jesus made no reply. He scorned to answer the governor's puppet, who thus hypocritically sought to challenge him.

The high priest made one more frantic effort.

"Are you the Christ, the Son of the Blessed One?" The Sadducees were very reluctant to utter the name of God; the First Book of Maccabees, a Sadducean book written a century earlier, never mentions the name of God. But with this question the high priest gave Jesus the opportunity to utter his great conviction, and he did not hesitate to reply.

"I am! and you will all see the Son of Man seated at the right hand of the Almighty, and coming in the clouds of the sky!"

This startling assertion gave the high priest all he wanted. He was sure he could get a conviction from the governor on this statement, but in a great pretense of horror and sorrow at such blasphemous words, he tore his clothes, oriental-fashion, and cried out to the council,

"What do we want of witnesses now? Did you hear his blasphemy? What is your decision?"

Thus put, the question was unanimously carried and the council condemned him to death. Yet Jewish scholars say that to claim to be Messiah was no crime in Jewish law, and think it more likely he was condemned for planning to destroy the temple, the charge on which the testimony did not agree, but which may have arisen from what he said about the certainty of its future destruction, as

preservation took the safer course. He denied it, and said to her,

"I don't know or understand what you mean."

Then he left the fire and went out into the gateway; perhaps he was thinking about leaving the place altogether, since it was beginning to look dangerous to stay around the palace. But the irrepressible girl caught sight of him out there, and seeing she had annoyed him started in again.

"This fellow is one of them," she proudly informed the bystanders.

Peter denied it again. But after a little while, they said to Peter,

"You certainly are one of them, for you're a Galilean!"

They had detected a Galilean tone in his speech. He was by now getting concerned, and began to swear with the strongest oaths he could think of, that he was nothing of the kind.

"I do not know this man you are talking about!" he declared.

But at that moment a cock crowed the second time, and Peter suddenly remembered what Jesus had said to him at the supper the night before: "Before the cock crows twice, you will disown me three times!" Sorrow for the loss of his Master, and the disappointment of all his high hopes, and most of all the revelation of the poor stuff of his own character, overwhelmed him, and he broke down and cried aloud.

This famous story of Peter's denials can only have come

Jesus' gloom at the supper had seemed to them little more than a momentary weakness. But now events were putting a somber meaning into his strange words.

The coming of daylight made it possible for the councilors to hold something like a regular meeting; the Sanhedrin never met at night, for then the gates of the temple were shut. Various irregularities about the trial of Jesus before the Sanhedrin have been pointed out. It was not held in the temple, where it always met; there is no parallel for a meeting at the high priest's house. A sentence of conviction could not be passed on the same day as the trial; it must go over to the next day; but the early morning meeting did not cover this point, for by the Jewish reckoning what we call Thursday night was a part not of Thursday but of Friday. The whole proceeding shows great precipitancy on the part of the council.

As soon as it was daylight, Jesus was duly condemned and bound, and, escorted by the council, was taken to the Roman governor, Pilate. For under the Romans, the Jews had no authority to impose and execute a sentence of death, which is what they demanded. This is Pilate's first appearance in the original gospel narrative, as Mark and Matthew reveal it. He had been governor of Judea for three or four years, having succeeded Valerius Gratus in A.D. 26. His residence was probably the palace Herod had built for himself in Jerusalem, in the middle of the west side of the city, near the present Jaffa gate.

It must have rudely disturbed the governor's comfortable routine to be called upon so early in the morning by his

Pilate seized the opportunity to suggest to them that they make Jesus their nominee, and asked them,

"Do you want me to set the king of the Jews free for you?" He was evidently convinced that Jesus was not likely to be a peril to public order in Judea. This would of course have defeated the plans of the high priests, and they instigated the newcomers to stick to their original purpose of getting him to set Barabbas free. When Pilate put it to a viva-voce vote, and asked them,

"Which of the two do you want me to release to you?" without hesitation they cried,

"Barabbas!"

Pilate pursued this play-acting at democratic action, probably hoping he could get them to vote for releasing Jesus too, and said,

"Then what shall I do with the man you call the king of the Jews?"

They shouted back, "Crucify him!"

Pilate was shocked himself at such ferocity, and tried to labor with them:

"Why, what has he done that is wrong?"

But they shouted all the louder, "Crucify him!"

Outwitted at his own game, Pilate could see no way to get around it. He wanted to satisfy the crowd, so he set Barabbas free, as they demanded, and after flogging Jesus, probably to weaken him so as to shorten his life, he handed him over to a squad of soldiers to be crucified. So casually and flippantly the thing was done.

whom his minions had already menaced in Galilee and in Trans-Jordan. He must have been relieved to see that Jesus was not John the Baptist, risen from the dead, as he had feared, but another man altogether.

But Mark's narrative proceeds with a stern restraint that is positively amazing. It is strangely objective; all the more poignant because no pity, no sympathy find expression in it. The soldiers took Jesus inside the courtyard of the Palace, and called the whole battalion together to see the man who was about to be executed. They dressed Jesus up in a red or purplish cloak, such as soldiers wore, made a wreath of thorns and crowned him with it, in mockery of his royalty, and shouted,

"Long live the king of the Jews!"

They struck him over the head with the stick, spat at him, and knelt down and pretended to do homage to him. Of course in a time when one emperor, Augustus, in his shows, had set ten thousand men to fighting each other to death to entertain the Roman public, life counted for very little. When the soldiers had finished making sport of him, they took off the purple cloak and put his own clothes back on him, and set out with him for the place of crucifixion.

This was probably north of the city, not far outside the wall, and they doubtless left the city by a gate near the present Damascus gate, though just what its name was is not certain. Jesus was weakened by the fearful flogging or scourging he had undergone, and it was not possible for him to keep up and carry the crossbeam of his cross to the place of execution, as the prisoner was expected to do. The

of board above his head, with his name and his crime chalked on it. It read,

"The king of the Jews."

Two robbers who were slated for execution were crucified at the same time, one at his right and one at his left, which increased if possible the degradation of his end. The place was near the highway, and people passing along on their ways to or from the city paused to jeer at the dying man. Mark describes them as acquainted with the charge against him, of meaning to tear down the temple and build one in three days.

"Come down from the cross," they shouted, "and save yourself!"

A delegation from the Sanhedrin was also in attendance, to see that their wishes were carried out. They exchanged satisfied comments upon the situation. A crucifixion was no such frightful novelty to them as it would be to us.

"He has saved others," they would say ironically, "but he can't save himself! Let this Christ, the king of Israel, come down from the cross now, so that we may see it and believe!"

Even the wretched men crucified with him found some relief in joining in his abuse.

We have seen that Peter is the most probable source for much if not all the material the Gospel of Mark preserves; he was the first apostle called, for he always outstripped his brother Andrew, and was evidently the spirited, expressive member of the pair; as we have seen, it was evidently he

picture in the Psalm, where God delivers his beloved out of the deepest despair.

There were no women present at the Last Supper, but of all Jesus' following only women, it would seem, stood by him to the end. And women have bulked largely in the Christian following ever since. This is no commonplace; look at its great rivals in the field of religion, Judaism, Mohammedanism! What have they for women? They are men's religions, and frankly so. And for that last terrible scene, the six hours of agony and delirium on the cross, we have only the memories of the women who at a little distance waited and listened.

And this, we must remember, was no peaceful deathbed; it was just as far from it as possible. Crucifixion was a death of torture. It is a pity modern faddists have picked the word up and taken out of it all its meaning, speaking lightly of "crucifying" one another! And too much must not be made of what the women and the bystanders understood Jesus was muttering or screaming from the cross. Even the words just quoted were differently understood by those near by. And later echoes from his lips found a place in the Gospel of Luke.

It was at three that the great cry from the twenty-second Psalm burst from his lips. But apparently before that, as Luke records it, one of the two thieves abused him, but the other reproved him, and asked Jesus to remember him when he came into his kingdom. Jesus answered,

"I tell you, you will be in Paradise with me today!"

And finally at three o'clock, Jesus said,

strong views, as we have seen, on the defilement produced by contact with the dead.

The Jews were accustomed to bury their dead immediately, on the day on which they died. It was in haste, therefore, and without the usual anointing that Jesus was taken down from the cross and carried off to burial. The Sabbath, moreover, was close at hand. But Joseph had a rock-cut tomb in the broken ground north of the city and not far from the place of the crucifixion. He bought a linen sheet, had Jesus taken down from the cross and wrapped in it, and then laid him in this tomb, which probably had room for two or more bodies, for it was entered by a doorway in the rock, before which a circular stone was rolled to serve as a door. The faithful Galilean women who had followed Jesus from Galilee, Mary of Magdala, and Mary, Joseph's mother, witnessed Joseph's action and followed Jesus' body to the tomb. They noted the spot, for they meant to come back after the Sabbath to bring spices and anoint his body.

For a little while the cruel death of Jesus must have seemed to those who loved and followed him the bitter, chilling end of all their hopes. It is one of the paradoxes of history, indeed the chief such paradox, that it was just the opposite. Our earliest account of the amazing sequel is from the hand of Paul, who twenty-five years later wrote to the Corinthians about it. He had told them of it years before, when he first visited Corinth in A.D. 50, for he regarded it as the most important thing he had to tell —how Jesus was raised from the dead and appeared, first

for us in the closing paragraphs of the Gospel of Matthew. Matthew, we can see, is faithfully copying everything of significance in Mark; he has done so from the very first, so that we can actually find fifteen-sixteenths of all Mark says reproduced in Matthew. Should this be thought an exaggeration, we may remember that Canon Streeter said he found nineteen-twentieths of Mark in Matthew! But in these closing pages particularly, while Matthew has much to add, he is meticulously incorporating into his narrative all that Mark affords. From Matthew 27:1 on, except for four or five scattered verses, hardly a clause or even a phrase of Mark's account is left out by Matthew. And where our Mark breaks off, Matthew goes right on with the story Mark has been leading up to—the reunion with Jesus at their rendezvous in Galilee. This has been specifically anticipated twice in the Gospel of Mark. Matthew tells how the eleven disciples went to Galilee, to the mountain to which Jesus had directed them. There they saw him and bowed down before him, though some were in doubt about it—a candid observation which in itself shows it was not a physical appearance. This is the appearance to the twelve mentioned by Paul in I Corinthians.

Then he gave them their great commission. He had confined his own work to his own people, the Jews. But the time has come to undertake the great mission, to the heathen world. They are to go and make disciples of all the heathen, and to teach them to observe all that he has commanded. And he will be with them always, to the very close of the age.

Paul, who had never seen him or heard him, in his bodily presence, caught from him his great sense that religion was not a legislation, and could not be reduced to one, and also caught his great vision of the love of God and love for men, of which John afterward made so much in John 3:16 and I John 4:8, 9. These passages owe much to Romans 5:5-8 and I Corinthians 13.

For the Gospel of John begins where Paul left off. It declares that Jesus has come back to trusting hearts as the Holy Spirit, the Comforter, the Helper, the Counselor, which would guide them into the full truth. The more Pharisaic idea, that Jesus' resurrection was a physical reanimation, played a very brief role in the serious thinking of the ancient church. After forty days, Luke declares, he ascended into the sky, the place, as Luke supposed, of heaven. But it was John's thought of his return, as an inward spiritual presence, that guided and inspired the primitive church and armed it with a spiritual force that was indomitable. It was another John, the Christian prophet of Ephesus, who felt that presence in his prison on the Island of Patmos. It was no arm of flesh on which the great figures of the later church leaned for support. Their most precious conviction was that they were actually "in Christ," in union with Christ, united to him, in communion and communication with him. It was this that purified their hearts and made them equal to any challenge or demand. Jesus had opened their way to God and they believed was still their great companion.

It was from this point of view that the Gospel of John

Names and Subjects

Quotations and References

THE OLD TESTAMENT